Habits of Highly Successful People: Cultivating Your Path to Success

Dhulia Bharat

Published by Dhulia Bharat, 2024.

While every precaution has been taken in the preparation of this book, the publisher assumes no responsibility for errors or omissions, or for damages resulting from the use of the information contained herein.

HABITS OF HIGHLY SUCCESSFUL PEOPLE: CULTIVATING YOUR PATH TO SUCCESS

First edition. April 2, 2024.

Copyright © 2024 Dhulia Bharat.

ISBN: 979-8224764471

Written by Dhulia Bharat.

Table of Contents

Chapter 1: Introduction

- Overview of the habits of highly successful people

Success is a goal that many people aspire to achieve in various aspects of their lives, whether it be in their career, relationships, or personal development. While success is defined differently by each individual, there are certain habits and traits that are commonly found in highly successful people. These habits are not just limited to financial success, but also include personal fulfillment and a sense of purpose in one's life.

One of the key habits of highly successful people is goal-setting. Successful individuals are known for setting specific, measurable, achievable, relevant, and time-bound goals for themselves. By having clear goals in mind, they are able to stay focused and motivated, as well as track their progress towards achieving their desired outcomes. Setting goals also helps successful people prioritize their tasks and allocate their time and resources effectively, leading to increased productivity and efficiency in their daily lives.

Another important habit of highly successful people is having a growth mindset. This mindset involves believing that one's abilities and intelligence can be developed through dedication and hard work, rather than being fixed traits. Successful individuals are resilient in the face of challenges and setbacks, viewing them as opportunities for learning and growth rather than insurmountable obstacles. By cultivating a growth mindset, highly successful people are able to adapt to change, embrace new opportunities, and continually improve themselves and their skills.

Additionally, highly successful people are known for their strong work ethic and discipline. They understand the importance of consistent effort and perseverance in achieving their goals, and are willing to put in the time and hard work necessary to succeed. Successful individuals are often early risers, making the most of their mornings to set the tone for a productive day ahead. They also prioritize self-care and wellbeing, incorporating exercise, healthy eating, and mindfulness practices into their daily routines to maintain their energy and focus.

Furthermore, highly successful people are adept at building and maintaining strong relationships. They understand the value of networking and surrounding themselves with supportive and like-minded individuals who share their goals and values. Successful individuals are skilled communicators, able to articulate their ideas clearly and persuasively, as well as listen actively and empathetically to others. They also prioritize gratitude and appreciation, recognizing and acknowledging the contributions of others to their success. By cultivating these habits in their daily lives, individuals can increase their chances of achieving success in both their personal and professional endeavors. Success is not a destination, but rather a journey that requires dedication, perseverance, and a willingness to continually learn and grow. By adopting the habits of highly successful people, anyone can unlock their full potential and create a fulfilling and meaningful life for themselves.

- Importance of cultivating beneficial habits

Cultivating beneficial habits is crucial for personal growth, success, and overall well-being. Habits are routines or behaviors that we engage in regularly, often without consciously thinking about them. Good habits can help us achieve our goals, improve our health, and enhance our quality of life. On the other hand, bad habits can hold us back, hinder our progress, and harm our physical and mental health. By intentionally cultivating positive habits and breaking free from negative ones, we can create a more fulfilling and meaningful life for ourselves.

One of the key benefits of cultivating beneficial habits is that they can increase our efficiency and productivity. When we have good habits in place, we are able to streamline our daily routines and avoid wasting time on unnecessary tasks. For example, developing a habit of creating to-do lists and prioritizing tasks can help us stay focused and organized throughout the day. Similarly, practicing good time management habits, such as setting aside specific blocks of time for work and leisure activities, can help us make the most of our time and achieve our goals more effectively.

Additionally, cultivating beneficial habits can have a positive impact on our physical health. For example, adopting a habit of regular exercise can improve our cardiovascular health, strengthen our muscles, and boost our immune system. Eating a balanced diet and drinking plenty of water are also healthy habits that can help us maintain a healthy weight, prevent chronic diseases, and feel more energetic throughout the day. By making small changes to our daily habits and routines, we can significantly improve our overall health and well-being in the long run.

Furthermore, cultivating beneficial habits can enhance our mental and emotional well-being. For example, practicing mindfulness and meditation can help us reduce stress, anxiety, and depression, and improve our ability to focus and concentrate. Developing a habit of gratitude can help us appreciate the positive aspects of our lives and cultivate a more positive outlook. Engaging in self-care activities, such as getting enough sleep, taking breaks when needed, and spending time with loved ones, can also help us recharge and rejuvenate our minds and bodies. By prioritizing our mental and emotional health and cultivating healthy habits, we can build resiliency, cope with challenges more effectively, and cultivate a greater sense of inner peace and contentment.

In addition to the personal benefits, cultivating beneficial habits can also have a positive impact on our relationships and social interactions. For example, developing a habit of active listening and showing empathy towards others can help us build stronger and more meaningful connections with people around us. Practicing good communication habits, such as sharing our thoughts and feelings openly and honestly, can help us resolve conflicts, build trust, and foster understanding in our relationships. By cultivating healthy habits in our interactions with others, we can create a more positive and harmonious social environment and contribute to a sense of community and belonging. By intentionally developing positive habits and breaking free from negative ones, we can improve our efficiency, productivity, physical health, mental and emotional well-being, and relationships. Cultivating beneficial habits is a lifelong process that requires self-awareness, commitment, and consistency. However, the rewards of cultivating healthy habits are well worth the effort, as they can help us live a more fulfilling, balanced, and meaningful life. By making small changes to our daily routines and behaviors, we can create a positive ripple effect that can transform our lives and the lives of those around us for the better.

Chapter 2: Setting Clear Goals

- The power of goal setting

Goal setting is a powerful tool that has been proven to enhance performance, motivation, and success in a variety of personal and professional endeavors. Setting specific, measurable, achievable, relevant, and time-bound goals provides individuals with a clear direction and purpose, allowing them to focus their efforts and energy on tasks that will move them closer to their desired outcomes. Research has shown that individuals who set goals are more likely to achieve higher levels of success and satisfaction in both their personal and professional lives.

One of the key benefits of goal setting is that it provides individuals with a roadmap for success. By setting specific and measurable goals, individuals are able to clearly define what they want to achieve and establish a plan for how to get there. This clarity allows individuals to prioritize their tasks and allocate their time and resources effectively, leading to increased productivity and efficiency. Additionally, setting achievable goals provides individuals with a sense of accomplishment as they make progress toward their objectives, which can boost motivation and confidence.

Furthermore, goal setting has been shown to increase focus and motivation. When individuals have clear goals to work toward, they are more likely to stay motivated and committed to their tasks, even in the face of obstacles or challenges. By setting specific and challenging goals, individuals can push themselves to reach new heights and achieve levels of success they may not have thought possible. This drive and determination can lead to improved performance and results, as individuals strive to meet and exceed their goals. Research has found that individuals who set goals are more likely to perform at higher levels and achieve better outcomes in various areas of their lives, including academics, career, and personal relationships. By setting clear and achievable goals, individuals can measure and track their progress, identify areas for improvement, and make adjustments as needed to stay on track. This process of continuous improvement can lead to increased success and satisfaction in all aspects of life.

Goal setting can also be a powerful tool for personal growth and development. By setting challenging goals that stretch individuals beyond their comfort zones, they can learn new skills, expand their knowledge, and develop new capabilities. Reaching these goals can build confidence and self-esteem, as individuals recognize their ability to overcome obstacles and achieve success. Setting goals can also provide individuals with a sense of purpose and direction, helping them to clarify their values and priorities and make choices that align with their long-term objectives. By setting specific, measurable, achievable, relevant, and time-bound goals, individuals can create a roadmap for success and focus their efforts and energy on tasks that will move them closer to their desired outcomes. Through goal setting, individuals can increase their focus and motivation, improve their performance, and promote personal growth and development.

- Strategies for setting and achieving goals

Setting and achieving goals is a vital aspect of personal and professional development. Without clear goals in mind, it can be challenging to stay focused and motivated on the path to success. In this article, we will explore some strategies for setting and achieving goals that can help individuals overcome obstacles and reach their desired outcomes.

One important strategy for setting and achieving goals is to ensure that they are specific and measurable. Instead of setting broad, vague goals like "improve productivity," it is more effective to set specific goals such as "increase productivity by 10% within three months. " This allows for a clear understanding of what needs to be achieved and provides a measurable benchmark for success. By setting specific and measurable goals, individuals can track their progress and make adjustments as needed to stay on track.

Another key strategy for setting and achieving goals is to prioritize and break them down into smaller, manageable tasks. It can be overwhelming to tackle a big goal all at once, so breaking it down into smaller steps can make it more achievable. By breaking goals into smaller tasks, individuals can focus on making progress one step at a time, which can help build momentum and keep motivation high. Prioritizing goals can also help individuals focus on what is most important and allocate their time and resources accordingly.

In addition to setting specific and measurable goals and breaking them down into smaller tasks, it is important to set realistic and achievable goals. Setting goals that are too ambitious or unrealistic can lead to frustration and disappointment if they are not achieved. It is important to set goals that stretch individuals beyond their comfort zone but are also within reach with effort and commitment. By setting realistic goals, individuals can build confidence as they achieve smaller victories along the way to their ultimate goal.

Furthermore, it is important to establish a timeline for achieving goals. Setting deadlines can create a sense of urgency and help individuals stay focused and committed to their goals. Without a timeline in place, goals can easily be pushed aside or forgotten, leading to a lack of progress. By setting realistic deadlines for each step of the goal-setting process, individuals can stay accountable and motivated to continue working towards their goals.

Another important strategy for setting and achieving goals is to regularly review and reassess progress. It is important to track progress towards goals and make adjustments as needed along the way. Instead of waiting until the deadline to evaluate progress, individuals should regularly review their goals and assess what is working well and what needs to be changed. By reviewing progress regularly, individuals can make informed decisions and course corrections to stay on track towards achieving their goals. By following these strategies for setting and achieving goals, individuals can overcome obstacles, stay focused, and ultimately reach their desired outcomes. By setting specific and measurable goals, breaking them down into smaller tasks, setting realistic timelines, and regularly reviewing progress, individuals can create a roadmap for success and achieve their goals with confidence and determination.

- **Examples of successful individuals and their goal-setting practices**

Goal setting is a key component of success for many individuals, both in their personal and professional lives. Setting goals provides direction, motivation, and a sense of accomplishment when those goals are achieved. It allows individuals to focus their efforts and resources on what is truly important to them and can help them stay on track towards achieving their desired outcomes. In this article, we will explore examples of successful individuals and the goal-setting practices that have played a significant role in their success.

One example of a successful individual who is known for their goal-setting practices is Oprah Winfrey. Oprah is a media mogul, philanthropist, and former talk show host who has achieved immense success in various fields. She is known for setting specific, measurable, achievable, relevant, and time-bound (SMART) goals for herself and for her businesses. Oprah sets high standards for herself and is constantly challenging herself to push beyond her limits. By setting ambitious goals and breaking them down into smaller, more manageable steps, Oprah has been able to achieve incredible success in her career.

Another example of a successful individual who is a proponent of goal setting is Elon Musk, the CEO of Tesla and SpaceX. Musk is a visionary entrepreneur who has set audacious goals for himself and his companies, from building electric cars to colonizing Mars. Musk is a firm believer in setting stretch goals that push the boundaries of what is possible and inspire his teams to think big. He is also known for his relentless work ethic and his ability to stay laser-focused on his goals, even in the face of setbacks and challenges. By setting bold, ambitious goals and staying committed to achieving them, Musk has been able to revolutionize industries and change the world in profound ways.

In addition to individuals like Oprah Winfrey and Elon Musk, many successful athletes also rely on goal-setting practices to achieve peak performance in their respective sports. One example is Serena Williams, one of the greatest tennis players of all time. Williams is known for setting specific, challenging goals for herself on the court, such as winning Grand Slam titles or regaining the number one ranking. She is also a master of visualization, using mental imagery to visualize herself achieving her goals and imagining the feeling of success. By setting clear, challenging goals and visualizing herself achieving them, Williams has been able to dominate the world of tennis and cement her legacy as one of the sport's all-time greats. By setting clear, specific goals that are challenging yet achievable, individuals can focus their efforts and resources on what truly matters to them and stay on track towards achieving their desired outcomes. Whether it's Oprah Winfrey setting ambitious goals for her media empire, Elon Musk aiming to revolutionize transportation and space exploration, or Serena Williams visualizing herself winning Grand Slam titles, successful individuals rely on goal-setting practices to drive their success. By emulating their example and adopting similar goal-setting practices in our own lives, we too can strive for greatness and achieve our dreams.

Chapter 3: Time Management and Prioritization

- Importance of effective time management

Time management is a critical skill that impacts every aspect of our lives, from personal to professional. Effectively managing our time allows us to prioritize tasks, stay organized, and ultimately achieve our goals efficiently and productively. In today's fast-paced world, where demands on our time are constantly increasing, it is more important than ever to master the art of time management.

One of the key reasons why effective time management is so important is that it allows us to make the most of the limited time we have each day. By setting clear goals and priorities, we can focus our energy on the tasks that are most important and avoid wasting time on activities that are not productive. This not only helps us to accomplish more in a shorter amount of time but also reduces stress and frustration by creating a sense of control and accomplishment.

Furthermore, effective time management helps us to avoid procrastination and distractions, which can derail our progress and prevent us from reaching our full potential. By breaking our tasks down into smaller, manageable chunks and setting deadlines for each, we can create a sense of urgency and motivation that keeps us on track and focused. This not only improves our productivity but also increases our sense of satisfaction and fulfillment as we see our goals being achieved.

In addition, effective time management allows us to create a better work-life balance, ensuring that we have time for both our professional responsibilities and personal interests. By allocating time for work, family, friends, and relaxation, we can avoid burnout and maintain a healthy and fulfilling life both inside and outside of the office. This balance is essential for our overall well-being and happiness, as it allows us to recharge and rejuvenate our minds and bodies, leading to increased energy and creativity in all aspects of our lives.

Moreover, effective time management helps us to improve our decision-making skills and problem-solving abilities. By carefully considering our priorities and deadlines, we can make informed choices about how to allocate our time and resources, leading to more efficient and effective outcomes. This ability to make quick and decisive decisions is crucial in today's fast-paced world, where opportunities and challenges arise at a moment's notice and require us to think on our feet.

All in all, effective time management is a key factor in achieving long-term success and reaching our full potential. By consistently managing our time well, we can develop strong habits and routines that become second nature, allowing us to maximize our productivity and optimize our performance. This not only helps us to achieve our short-term goals but also sets us up for success in the long run, as we build a reputation for reliability, effectiveness, and efficiency that can open doors to new opportunities and career advancements. By mastering this skill, we can prioritize our tasks, stay organized, and achieve our goals efficiently and productively. This not only leads to increased satisfaction and fulfillment but also helps us to avoid procrastination and distractions, maintain a healthy work-life balance, improve our decision-making skills, and ultimately reach our full potential. So, take control of your time today, and watch as your productivity and success soar to new heights.

- Techniques for prioritizing tasks

Prioritizing tasks is a critical skill for achieving productivity and efficiency in any professional or academic setting. With the ever-increasing demands on our time and energy, it is essential to develop effective techniques for determining which tasks are most important and should be addressed first. In this discussion, we will explore several proven strategies for prioritizing tasks, including the Eisenhower Matrix, the ABCDE method, and the Pomodoro Technique.

One of the most popular and effective methods for prioritizing tasks is the Eisenhower Matrix. This technique, named after former US President Dwight D. Eisenhower, involves categorizing tasks into four quadrants based on their importance and urgency. Quadrant 1 includes tasks that are both important and urgent and should be addressed immediately. Quadrant 2 includes tasks that are important but not urgent, requiring careful planning and scheduling. Quadrant 3 includes tasks that are urgent but not important, often distractions that can be delegated or eliminated. To draw to a close, Quadrant 4 includes tasks that are neither important nor urgent and can be safely ignored. By using the Eisenhower Matrix, individuals can quickly identify which tasks require immediate attention and which can be deferred or eliminated altogether.

Another useful method for prioritizing tasks is the ABCDE method, popularized by time management expert Brian Tracy. In this approach, tasks are assigned a priority level based on their importance and deadlines. Tasks are labeled as A, B, or C, with A tasks being the most important and requiring immediate action, B tasks being important but not urgent, and C tasks being less important and can be done at a later time. Additionally, tasks can be further categorized into D tasks, which can be delegated to others, and E tasks, which can be eliminated entirely. By using the ABCDE method, individuals can focus on completing high-priority tasks first while effectively managing their time and resources.

To draw to a close, the Pomodoro Technique is a popular time management strategy that can be used to prioritize tasks and improve focus and productivity. This technique involves breaking work into short, focused intervals called Pomodoros, typically 25 minutes, followed by a short break. During each Pomodoro, individuals focus on a single task without distractions, aiming to complete as much work as possible before the break. By using the Pomodoro Technique, individuals can prioritize tasks based on their importance and deadlines, focusing on completing high-priority tasks first while maintaining a high level of concentration and productivity. By using effective techniques such as the Eisenhower Matrix, the ABCDE method, and the Pomodoro Technique, individuals can identify which tasks are most important and require immediate attention, while managing their time and resources effectively. By mastering these prioritization techniques, individuals can improve their focus, productivity, and overall success in their personal and professional lives.

- Balancing work, personal life, and self-care

Balancing work, personal life, and self-care is essential for maintaining overall well-being and productivity. In today's fast-paced and demanding world, many people struggle to find a harmonious equilibrium between their professional responsibilities, personal commitments, and taking time to care for themselves. However, it is crucial to recognize that neglecting any one of these areas can lead to burnout, increased stress, and a decline in mental and physical health.

One of the keys to successfully balancing work, personal life, and self-care is effective time management. Prioritizing tasks, setting realistic goals, and creating a schedule that allows for dedicated time to focus on work, personal relationships, and self-care activities is vital. By allocating specific blocks of time for each area of your life, you can ensure that nothing gets overlooked or neglected. Additionally, practicing mindfulness and being present in the moment can help you make the most of your time and prevent feelings of overwhelm.

Another important aspect of achieving balance is setting boundaries. It is crucial to establish clear boundaries between work and personal time to prevent them from bleeding into each other. This means turning off work-related notifications outside of business hours, setting limits on how much time you spend on work tasks at home, and prioritizing quality time with loved ones without distractions. By honoring these boundaries, you can maintain a healthy separation between your professional and personal life, leading to improved overall well-being.

Self-care is often the first thing to go when life gets busy, but it is crucial for maintaining your physical, mental, and emotional health. Taking time to care for yourself is not selfish; it is necessary for replenishing your energy, reducing stress, and enhancing your overall quality of life. Self-care activities can include exercise, meditation, spending time in nature, engaging in hobbies, and practicing gratitude. Finding activities that bring you joy and relaxation is key to creating a self-care routine that works for you.

It is also essential to seek support from others when trying to balance work, personal life, and self-care. Whether it be reaching out to friends and family for help with tasks, seeking advice from a mentor or coach, or enlisting the support of a therapist or counselor, having a strong support system can make a significant difference in your ability to juggle the various demands of life. Don't be afraid to ask for help when you need it or delegate tasks to others to lighten your load. By recognizing the importance of each of these areas and making them a priority in your life, you can create a harmonious equilibrium that allows you to thrive in all aspects of your life. Remember that finding balance is an ongoing process that requires flexibility, self-awareness, and a willingness to make adjustments as needed. Prioritize your well-being and make time for what truly matters to you – your work, personal relationships, and most importantly, yourself.

Chapter 4: Building a Growth Mindset

- Understanding the concept of a growth mindset

A growth mindset is a psychological theory developed by psychologist Carol Dweck that describes the belief that one's abilities and intelligence can be developed and improved over time through effort, persistence, and learning. This concept contrasts with a fixed mindset, which is the belief that one's abilities are innate and cannot be changed. People with a growth mindset are more likely to embrace challenges, learn from failures, and see effort as a pathway to success. This mindset has important implications for personal development, academic achievement, and overall well-being.

One of the key characteristics of a growth mindset is the belief that intelligence and abilities can be developed through hard work and dedication. People with a growth mindset view challenges as opportunities to learn and grow, rather than as threats to their self-esteem or intelligence. They understand that setbacks and failures are a natural part of the learning process and are willing to put in the effort to overcome obstacles and improve their skills. This attitude not only leads to increased motivation and resilience but also fosters a sense of curiosity and a willingness to explore new ideas and experiences.

In contrast, individuals with a fixed mindset believe that their abilities are predetermined and cannot be changed. They are more likely to avoid challenges, give up easily in the face of setbacks, and view effort as fruitless. This mindset can lead to a fear of failure, a lack of motivation to learn and grow, and a limited sense of potential. People with a fixed mindset may shy away from new experiences or opportunities for growth, as they fear that they will not be able to succeed or meet their own high standards. This can result in missed opportunities for learning, personal development, and achievement.

Research has shown that individuals with a growth mindset tend to outperform those with a fixed mindset in a variety of areas, including academics, athletics, and professional success. This is because a growth mindset fosters a love of learning, a willingness to take risks, and a belief in one's ability to improve over time. People with a growth mindset are more likely to seek out feedback and constructive criticism, as they see these as opportunities to learn and grow. They are also more likely to persevere in the face of obstacles and setbacks, as they view these challenges as temporary and surmountable.

There are several ways to cultivate a growth mindset and reap its benefits in your own life. One of the first steps is to become aware of your own beliefs about intelligence and abilities. Pay attention to the way you speak to yourself and others about success, failure, and effort. Notice if you tend to attribute your achievements or setbacks to innate talent or external factors, rather than to your own hard work and dedication. Challenge yourself to reframe these beliefs and cultivate a more growth-oriented mindset.

Another important aspect of developing a growth mindset is to embrace challenges and view them as opportunities for growth and learning. Instead of shying away from difficult tasks or situations, approach them with curiosity and a willingness to learn. Seek out feedback and constructive criticism from others, as this can help you identify areas for improvement and enhance your skills. Remember that setbacks and failures are a natural part of the learning process and do not define your intelligence or abilities. Instead, see them as valuable opportunities to learn, grow, and improve.

To conclude, it is important to cultivate a sense of resilience and perseverance in the face of obstacles and setbacks. Adopt a positive attitude towards challenges and setbacks, and remember that they are not a reflection of your worth or intelligence. Instead, see them as opportunities to learn, grow, and become more resilient. Focus on the progress you have made and the lessons you have learned, rather than dwelling on past failures or mistakes. With a growth mindset, you can approach challenges with confidence, curiosity, and a belief in your own ability to learn and improve over time.

- Strategies for developing a growth mindset

Developing a growth mindset is an essential component of personal and professional growth. It involves recognizing that abilities and intelligence can be developed and improved with effort and perseverance. People with a growth mindset believe that they can learn and improve, rather than believing that intelligence is fixed. This mindset is associated with greater resilience, motivation, and success in various areas of life, including academics, careers, and relationships.

One strategy for developing a growth mindset is to embrace challenges. Instead of avoiding difficult tasks or situations, individuals with a growth mindset see them as opportunities for learning and growth. They understand that challenges help them develop new skills and improve their abilities. By taking on challenging tasks, people can expand their comfort zone and push themselves to achieve new levels of success. This attitude can lead to increased confidence and a willingness to take on new challenges in the future.

Another strategy for developing a growth mindset is to view failures as learning experiences. Instead of seeing failure as a sign of incompetence or lack of ability, individuals with a growth mindset see it as an opportunity to learn and grow. They understand that setbacks are a natural part of the learning process and that they can be valuable lessons that can help them improve in the future. By reframing failure as a stepping stone to success, people can bounce back more quickly and continue to progress toward their goals.

A third strategy for developing a growth mindset is to cultivate a sense of curiosity and openness to new experiences. People with a growth mindset are constantly seeking out new information, ideas, and perspectives. They are open to feedback and willing to learn from others. By being curious and open-minded, individuals can expand their knowledge and skills, making them more adaptable and resilient in the face of challenges. This can also lead to greater creativity and innovation, as people are more willing to take risks and explore novel ideas.

Additionally, developing a growth mindset involves cultivating a sense of perseverance and grit. People with a growth mindset understand that progress takes time and effort, and that success is not always immediate. They are willing to put in the hard work and persist through setbacks and obstacles in order to achieve their goals. By developing a strong work ethic and a sense of determination, individuals can overcome challenges and continue to grow and improve over time. By embracing challenges, viewing failures as learning opportunities, cultivating curiosity and openness, and developing perseverance and grit, individuals can unlock their full potential and achieve greater success in various areas of life. By adopting these strategies and mindset, people can build resilience, motivation, and a willingness to learn and grow, ultimately leading to a more fulfilling and successful life.

- Examples of successful individuals who embody a growth mindset

A growth mindset is a belief that one's abilities and intelligence can be developed over time through hard work, perseverance, and learning from failure. Individuals who possess a growth mindset are more likely to embrace challenges, take risks, and see failures as opportunities to learn and grow. This mindset is associated with increased motivation, resilience, and overall success in various areas of life.

One example of a successful individual who embodies a growth mindset is Elon Musk, the CEO of Tesla and SpaceX. Musk is known for his ambitious goals and willingness to take risks in pursuit of his vision for the future. Despite facing numerous setbacks and challenges in his career, Musk has remained resilient and focused on continuously learning and improving. He has credited his success to his belief in the power of hard work, perseverance, and the willingness to innovate and adapt in the face of adversity.

Another example of a successful individual with a growth mindset is Oprah Winfrey, media mogul and philanthropist. Winfrey's rise to success was not without its share of challenges, including a difficult childhood and struggles with poverty. However, she never allowed these obstacles to deter her from pursuing her dreams and making a positive impact on the world. Winfrey's commitment to personal growth, self-improvement, and learning from her experiences has been instrumental in her success and influence.

A third example of a successful individual who embodies a growth mindset is LeBron James, professional basketball player and entrepreneur. James is widely regarded as one of the greatest basketball players of all time, but his success is not solely attributed to his natural talent. James is known for his relentless work ethic, commitment to continuous improvement, and willingness to push himself outside of his comfort zone. He has embraced challenges, overcome setbacks, and maintained a growth mindset throughout his career, which has set him apart as a true leader both on and off the court. By embracing challenges, taking risks, and learning from failure, these individuals are able to continually improve and grow, ultimately realizing their full potential. Elon Musk, Oprah Winfrey, and LeBron James are just a few examples of successful individuals who have demonstrated the power of a growth mindset in achieving their goals and making a positive impact on the world. As we strive to reach our own aspirations, we can look to these role models for inspiration and guidance in cultivating a mindset that fosters growth, resilience, and success.

Chapter 5: Continuous Learning and Personal Development

- Benefits of lifelong learning

Lifelong learning is a crucial aspect of personal development that not only enhances your knowledge and skills but also plays a significant role in maintaining competitiveness in the ever-evolving job market. The benefits of lifelong learning are numerous and far-reaching, impacting various aspects of your life both personally and professionally.

One of the key advantages of lifelong learning is the opportunity to stay relevant and competitive in your chosen field. As technology and industries continue to evolve at a rapid pace, it is essential to continuously update your knowledge and skills to keep up with these changes. Lifelong learning allows you to adapt to new trends and developments, ensuring that you remain marketable and employable throughout your career. By continuously seeking out new knowledge and skills, you can improve your performance at work, leading to greater job satisfaction and potentially opening up new opportunities for advancement. Employers often value employees who demonstrate a commitment to learning and self-improvement, as they are more likely to bring fresh ideas and perspectives to the table.

In addition to enhancing your career prospects, lifelong learning can also have a positive impact on your personal growth and well-being. Learning new things can boost your confidence and self-esteem, as you gain a sense of accomplishment from acquiring new skills and knowledge.

Moreover, lifelong learning can also help you stay intellectually sharp and engaged as you age. Keeping your brain stimulated through continuous learning can help prevent cognitive decline and improve memory and concentration. It can also provide a sense of purpose and fulfillment as you age, allowing you to remain active and engaged in the world around you.

So, whether you choose to pursue formal education, attend workshops and seminars, or simply engage in self-directed learning, the benefits of lifelong learning are undeniable.

- Ways to continuously improve oneself

Self-improvement is a lifelong journey that requires dedication, self-awareness, and a growth mindset. There are several ways to continuously improve oneself, both personally and professionally, in order to reach our full potential and live a fulfilling life. By setting goals, cultivating new skills, seeking feedback, and practicing self-reflection, individuals can develop a growth mindset that allows them to adapt, learn, and grow over time. In this article, we will explore some practical strategies for personal and professional development that can help individuals enhance their knowledge, skills, and overall well-being.

Setting specific, measurable, achievable, relevant, and time-bound (SMART) goals is a crucial first step in self-improvement. By identifying areas for growth and creating a roadmap for success, individuals can focus their efforts on areas that will have the greatest impact on their personal and professional development. Whether it's learning a new language, improving time management skills, or advancing in a career, setting SMART goals provides direction and motivation to stay on track and make meaningful progress. Additionally, breaking larger goals down into smaller, more manageable tasks can help individuals build momentum, stay motivated, and celebrate incremental successes along the way.

In addition to setting goals, cultivating new skills is another key aspect of continuous self-improvement. Whether it's through formal education, vocational training, workshops, or self-directed learning, acquiring new skills can broaden one's knowledge base, enhance problem-solving abilities, and open up new opportunities for personal and professional growth. In today's rapidly changing world, staying current with industry trends and technological advancements is essential for remaining competitive and adaptable in the workplace. By actively seeking out opportunities to learn new skills, individuals can expand their capabilities, boost their confidence, and position themselves for success in a dynamic and evolving job market.

Seeking feedback from others is another valuable strategy for self-improvement. Whether it's from colleagues, mentors, friends, or family members, soliciting feedback can provide valuable insights, perspectives, and constructive criticism that can help individuals identify blind spots, recognize areas for improvement, and make informed decisions about their personal and professional development. In addition, feedback can help individuals build stronger relationships, foster a culture of open communication, and cultivate a growth mindset that values continuous learning and improvement. By actively seeking out feedback, individuals can gain valuable insights into their strengths and weaknesses, receive guidance on how to improve, and develop a greater sense of self-awareness that can lead to long-term success.

Practicing self-reflection is another effective way to continuously improve oneself. By taking the time to reflect on past experiences, accomplishments, failures, and challenges, individuals can gain valuable insights into their values, beliefs, motivations, and goals. Self-reflection can help individuals identify patterns of behavior, thought, and emotion that may be holding them back from reaching their full potential. By examining past decisions, actions, and outcomes, individuals can learn from their mistakes, make adjustments, and develop new strategies for success. In addition, self-reflection can help individuals develop a growth mindset, cultivate resilience, and build emotional intelligence that can enhance their personal and professional relationships.

Building a strong support network is also essential for continuous self-improvement. By surrounding oneself with positive, motivated, and supportive individuals, individuals can draw inspiration, encouragement, and guidance from others who share similar goals, values, and aspirations. Whether it's joining a professional organization, attending networking events, or participating in mentorship programs, building a strong support network can provide individuals with valuable resources, connections, and opportunities for growth and development. Additionally, collaborating with others, sharing ideas, and receiving support can help individuals overcome challenges, break through barriers, and achieve their personal and professional goals. By setting goals, cultivating new skills, seeking feedback, practicing self-reflection, and building a strong support network, individuals can enhance their knowledge, skills, and overall well-being. Through continuous learning, adaptation, and growth, individuals can unlock their full potential, achieve their goals, and lead a fulfilling and meaningful life. By embracing a proactive approach to personal and professional development, individuals can position themselves for success in a competitive and ever-changing world.

- Resources for personal and professional development

Personal and professional development are essential aspects of growth and success in both our personal and professional lives. It is crucial to continuously develop and improve oneself in order to reach our full potential and achieve our goals. Fortunately, there are a wide range of resources available to help individuals in their journey of personal and professional development. These resources can come in many forms, including books, online courses, workshops, coaching, and mentorship programs.

One of the most accessible and widely used resources for personal and professional development is books. There are countless books available on a variety of topics including leadership, communication skills, time management, goal setting, and personal growth. Books provide valuable insights, strategies, and tips that can help individuals develop new skills, improve their performance, and achieve their goals. Some popular books on personal development include "The 7 Habits of Highly Effective People" by Stephen Covey, "Mindset: The New Psychology of Success" by Carol Dweck, and "How to Win Friends and Influence People" by Dale Carnegie.

In addition to books, online courses have become increasingly popular as a resource for personal and professional development. Online courses offer the convenience of learning from the comfort of one's own home and at one's own pace. There are a multitude of online platforms that offer courses on a wide range of topics, from business and entrepreneurship to personal finance and mindfulness. Some popular online learning platforms include Coursera, Udemy, and LinkedIn Learning. These courses are taught by experts in their respective fields and provide valuable knowledge and skills that can help individuals advance in their careers and personal lives.

Another valuable resource for personal and professional development is workshops and seminars. These events provide opportunities for individuals to learn new skills, network with like-minded individuals, and gain valuable insights from experts in their respective fields. Workshops and seminars cover a variety of topics, including leadership development, communication skills, emotional intelligence, and conflict resolution. Attending these events can help individuals expand their knowledge, build their confidence, and enhance their personal and professional growth.

Coaching and mentorship programs are another valuable resource for personal and professional development. Coaches and mentors provide guidance, support, and accountability to individuals seeking to improve themselves and achieve their goals. Coaches work one-on-one with individuals to help them set and achieve specific goals, overcome obstacles, and develop new skills. Mentors, on the other hand, provide guidance and advice based on their own experiences and expertise. Both coaching and mentorship programs can be invaluable tools for personal and professional development. Fortunately, there are a wide range of resources available to help individuals in their journey of self-improvement, including books, online courses, workshops, coaching, and mentorship programs. By taking advantage of these resources and investing in one's own growth and development, individuals can enhance their skills, advance in their careers, and lead more fulfilling lives.

Chapter 6: Building Positive Relationships

- The importance of cultivating positive relationships

Positive relationships play a crucial role in our personal and professional lives. The way we interact with others can greatly impact our well-being, success, and overall happiness. Cultivating positive relationships involves building strong connections with others based on trust, respect, communication, and mutual support. These relationships can have a profound effect on various aspects of our lives, including our mental and emotional health, career advancement, and overall satisfaction with life.

One of the key advantages of cultivating positive relationships is the impact it can have on our mental and emotional well-being. Research has shown that having healthy relationships with others can improve our overall mental health and reduce feelings of loneliness, anxiety, and depression. Positive relationships provide us with a support system that can help us navigate life's challenges and cope with stress. By surrounding ourselves with people who uplift and encourage us, we can create a sense of belonging and connection that is essential for our emotional well-being.

In addition to benefiting our mental and emotional health, positive relationships can also have a significant impact on our professional lives. Building strong connections with colleagues, mentors, and clients can lead to increased collaboration, productivity, and job satisfaction. When we have positive relationships with those we work with, we are more likely to communicate effectively, resolve conflicts amicably, and work together towards common goals. These relationships can also help us build our professional network and open up opportunities for career advancement and growth.

Furthermore, cultivating positive relationships can enhance our overall satisfaction with life. Research has shown that people who have strong social connections and supportive relationships tend to be happier and more fulfilled. By investing time and effort into building positive relationships with family, friends, and colleagues, we can create a sense of purpose and meaning in our lives. These relationships provide us with a sense of belonging, love, and support that can improve our overall quality of life and well-being.

In order to cultivate positive relationships, it is important to prioritize communication, empathy, and mutual respect. Good communication is essential for building strong connections with others, as it helps us understand each other's thoughts, feelings, and needs. By actively listening and expressing ourselves effectively, we can foster trust and understanding in our relationships. Empathy is also vital for cultivating positive relationships, as it allows us to relate to and understand the experiences of others. By showing compassion and empathy towards others, we can build stronger bonds and create a sense of trust and connection.

Moreover, mutual respect is fundamental for maintaining positive relationships. Respecting others' boundaries, opinions, and feelings demonstrates that we value and appreciate them as individuals. By treating others with kindness, consideration, and respect, we can build trusting and supportive relationships that are based on mutual understanding and appreciation. When we cultivate positive relationships built on communication, empathy, and respect, we create a foundation for lasting and meaningful connections that can enrich our lives and contribute to our overall well-being. Building strong connections with others based on trust, respect, communication, and support can have a profound impact on our mental and emotional health, career advancement, and overall satisfaction with life. By prioritizing communication, empathy, and mutual respect in our relationships, we can create a sense of belonging, purpose, and fulfillment that enriches our lives and enhances our well-being. Investing time and effort into building positive relationships with family, friends, and colleagues can lead to greater happiness, success, and overall well-being in all areas of our lives.

- Communication skills for fostering strong connections

Communication skills are essential for fostering strong connections and building successful relationships both personally and professionally. Effective communication is the foundation of any healthy relationship, as it allows individuals to express their thoughts, feelings, and needs in a clear and respectful manner. By improving our communication skills, we can enhance our ability to connect with others on a deeper level, build trust and understanding, and resolve conflicts more effectively.

One key aspect of communication skills is active listening. Active listening involves not only hearing what the other person is saying, but also paying attention to their body language, tone of voice, and emotions. By truly listening to the other person, we can show them that we value and respect their thoughts and feelings. This can help to foster a sense of trust and understanding in the relationship, leading to stronger connections and deeper levels of communication.

Another important communication skill for fostering strong connections is empathy. Empathy involves putting ourselves in the other person's shoes and trying to understand their perspective and feelings. By showing empathy towards others, we can demonstrate that we care about their well-being and are willing to support them in times of need. This can help to build stronger connections and create a sense of mutual understanding and respect in the relationship.

Effective communication also involves being able to express ourselves clearly and assertively. Assertive communication involves being able to communicate our thoughts, feelings, and needs in a direct and respectful manner. By expressing ourselves assertively, we can avoid misunderstandings and conflicts, and ensure that our message is received and understood by the other person. This can help to build trust and respect in the relationship, and foster stronger connections based on open and honest communication.

In addition to active listening, empathy, and assertive communication, another important aspect of communication skills for fostering strong connections is nonverbal communication. Nonverbal communication includes facial expressions, body language, and tone of voice, and can often convey more meaning than words alone. By being aware of our nonverbal cues and adjusting them to match our verbal communication, we can enhance our ability to connect with others and build stronger relationships based on mutual understanding and trust. By improving our active listening, empathy, assertive communication, and nonverbal communication skills, we can enhance our ability to connect with others on a deeper level, build trust and understanding, and resolve conflicts more effectively. By cultivating these communication skills, we can create stronger connections, enhance our relationships, and lead more fulfilling and meaningful lives.

- Examples of successful people who prioritize relationships

Successful people understand the importance of prioritizing relationships in both their personal and professional lives. These individuals recognize that cultivating strong connections with others can lead to increased opportunities, enhanced collaboration, and a more fulfilling life overall. One prime example of successful individuals who prioritize relationships is Warren Buffett, the renowned investor and philanthropist. Buffett is known for his ability to build enduring relationships with his business partners, employees, and the companies in which he invests. His emphasis on maintaining strong connections has played a significant role in his success as one of the world's wealthiest individuals.

Another notable example of a successful person who values relationships is Oprah Winfrey, the media mogul and philanthropist. Winfrey has built an empire based on her ability to connect with and inspire others through her television shows, books, and philanthropic endeavors. She attributes much of her success to the meaningful relationships she has cultivated over the years, emphasizing the importance of authenticity, empathy, and respect in all interactions. Winfrey's dedication to building and nurturing connections with others has not only contributed to her professional success but has also made her a respected and admired figure in the entertainment industry.

In the tech industry, Mark Zuckerberg, the co-founder and CEO of Facebook, is a prime example of a successful individual who prioritizes relationships. Zuckerberg is known for his focus on building strong relationships with his employees, investors, and users. He emphasizes open communication, transparency, and collaboration as key components of building successful relationships both within his company and with external partners.

Zuckerberg's ability to connect with others and rally support for his vision has been instrumental in the growth and success of Facebook as one of the world's largest social media platforms.

In the world of sports, Serena Williams, the legendary tennis player, is another example of a successful person who values relationships. Williams has not only achieved unparalleled success on the tennis court but has also built strong connections with her fellow athletes, sponsors, and fans. She attributes much of her success to the support and encouragement of her family, coaches, and teammates, emphasizing the importance of surrounding oneself with positive and empowering relationships. Williams' ability to foster strong connections with others has not only propelled her to multiple Grand Slam titles but has also made her a role model and inspiration to countless individuals around the world.

Successful people understand that relationships are the foundation of success in both their personal and professional lives. By prioritizing meaningful connections with others, individuals can build a strong support network, access new opportunities, and create a more fulfilling and rewarding life. Whether it be in the business world, entertainment industry, tech sector, or sports arena, examples abound of successful individuals who have leveraged their relationships to achieve their goals and make a positive impact on the world. By following in the footsteps of these successful individuals and emphasizing the importance of relationships, anyone can unlock their full potential and reach new heights of success and fulfillment.

Chapter 7: Overcoming Obstacles and Resilience

- Strategies for overcoming challenges

Challenges are an inevitable part of life, and they often present themselves in various forms, whether they be personal, professional, or academic. It is essential to have effective strategies in place to overcome these challenges and navigate through them successfully. In this essay, we will explore some key strategies that can help individuals overcome obstacles and achieve their goals.

First and foremost, it is important to have a positive mindset when facing challenges. A positive attitude can make a significant difference in how we perceive and approach obstacles. By maintaining a hopeful and optimistic outlook, we can better tackle challenges and find solutions to overcome them. It is crucial to remind ourselves that challenges are opportunities for growth and development, and that setbacks are a natural part of the process of achieving success.

Another important strategy for overcoming challenges is to break them down into smaller, more manageable tasks. When faced with a daunting obstacle, it can be overwhelming to try to tackle it all at once. By breaking the challenge into smaller, bite-sized tasks, we can make the problem more manageable and approach it one step at a time. This approach can help us to stay focused and motivated, and can ultimately lead to a more successful outcome.

It is also important to seek support and guidance from others when facing challenges. Whether it be friends, family, colleagues, or mentors, having a support system in place can make a significant difference in our ability to overcome obstacles. By reaching out to others for advice, encouragement, or emotional support, we can gain valuable insights and perspectives that can help us navigate through challenges more effectively. Additionally, having a support system can provide us with a sense of belonging and connection, which can boost our resilience and determination.

Furthermore, it is important to learn from our mistakes and failures when faced with challenges. It is natural to experience setbacks and roadblocks along the way, but it is how we respond to these setbacks that can make a difference in our ability to overcome challenges. By reflecting on what went wrong, identifying areas for improvement, and learning from our mistakes, we can grow stronger and more resilient in the face of future challenges. Embracing failure as a learning opportunity can help us to develop a growth mindset and adapt to new situations more effectively.

In addition, it is crucial to stay flexible and adaptable when facing challenges. Oftentimes, obstacles can arise unexpectedly, and it is important to be able to adjust our plans and strategies accordingly. By remaining open to new possibilities and willing to pivot when necessary, we can better navigate through challenges and find innovative solutions to overcome them. Flexibility and adaptability are key traits of successful individuals who are able to overcome obstacles and achieve their goals.

Lastly, it is important to practice self-care and prioritize our well-being when facing challenges. It can be easy to neglect our physical, emotional, and mental health when dealing with obstacles, but taking care of ourselves is essential for maintaining a strong and resilient mindset. By practicing self-care activities such as exercise, meditation, journaling, or spending time with loved ones, we can recharge our batteries and stay mentally and emotionally balanced when facing challenges. Prioritizing our well-being not only helps us to overcome obstacles more effectively, but also allows us to sustain our energy and motivation in the long run. By maintaining a positive mindset, breaking challenges into smaller tasks, seeking support from others, learning from our mistakes, staying flexible and adaptable, and prioritizing our well-being, we can navigate through obstacles with resilience and determination. With perseverance, resilience, and a growth mindset, we can overcome challenges and emerge stronger and more successful on the other side.

- Building resilience in the face of adversity

Building resilience in the face of adversity is a critical skill that can help individuals navigate life's challenges with strength and perseverance. Resilience is defined as the ability to bounce back from setbacks and adapt to difficult situations. It is a key component of mental well-being and can help individuals cope with stress, trauma, and other negative life events. Resilient individuals are better equipped to handle setbacks and thrive in the face of adversity.

There are several factors that contribute to building resilience. One of the most important factors is having a strong support system. Friends, family, and other close relationships can provide emotional support during difficult times and help individuals feel connected and valued. Building and maintaining these relationships is critical to resilience. Studies have shown that individuals with strong social support networks are better able to cope with stress and bounce back from adversity.

Another important factor in building resilience is developing a positive outlook. Optimism and a belief in one's ability to overcome challenges can help individuals maintain perspective and stay hopeful in the face of adversity. Practicing gratitude, focusing on strengths, and reframing negative thoughts can all contribute to a more positive mindset. Research has shown that individuals with a positive outlook are more likely to bounce back from setbacks and experience greater well-being.

In addition to social support and a positive outlook, resilience can also be strengthened through self-care and self-awareness. Taking care of one's physical, emotional, and mental health is essential for building resilience. This includes getting enough sleep, eating well, exercising regularly, and engaging in activities that bring joy and relaxation. Self-awareness, or the ability to recognize and regulate emotions, is also important for resilience. By developing mindfulness and emotional intelligence skills, individuals can better cope with stress and manage their reactions to challenging situations.

Resilience is not only important for individuals, but also for organizations and communities. Building resilience at the organizational level involves establishing clear communication channels, fostering a supportive work environment, and providing resources for employees to cope with stress and adversity. By promoting a culture of resilience, organizations can better adapt to change and thrive in the face of challenges. Similarly, communities can build resilience by investing in social support networks, providing resources for mental health and well-being, and fostering a sense of belonging and connectedness. By cultivating social support, fostering a positive outlook, practicing self-care, and developing self-awareness, individuals can strengthen their resilience and enhance their well-being. Resilience is not only important for individuals, but also for organizations and communities. By promoting resilience at all levels, we can better cope with stress, adapt to change, and thrive in the face of adversity.

- Real-life examples of individuals who have overcome obstacles

In life, we often face obstacles that can seem insurmountable. Whether it be personal challenges, professional setbacks, or societal barriers, overcoming obstacles requires resilience, determination, and a positive mindset. However, it is important to remember that overcoming obstacles is possible, and there are countless examples of individuals who have persevered in the face of adversity.

One powerful example of overcoming obstacles is that of Oprah Winfrey. Born into poverty in rural Mississippi, Oprah faced numerous challenges throughout her childhood, including being sexually abused and living in extreme poverty. Despite these obstacles, Oprah managed to excel in school and earn a scholarship to college. She went on to become one of the most successful media moguls in history, building a multi-billion dollar empire through her television show, magazine, and production company. Oprah's story is a reminder that no matter where you come from or what challenges you face, it is possible to achieve success through hard work, perseverance, and belief in oneself.

Another inspirational example of overcoming obstacles is that of J. K. Rowling, the author of the Harry Potter series. Rowling faced a myriad of challenges before she found success as a writer, including poverty, divorce, and depression. At one point, she was a single mother struggling to make ends meet, rejected by numerous publishers who saw no potential in her manuscript. Despite these setbacks, Rowling never gave up on her dream of being a writer. To finish, after much perseverance and determination, Rowling found a publisher who believed in her work, and the rest, as they say, is history. The Harry Potter series went on to become one of the best-selling book franchises of all time, solidifying Rowling's place as one of the most successful authors in the world.

One more real-life example of overcoming obstacles is that of Malala Yousafzai, the youngest Nobel Prize laureate in history. Malala grew up in Pakistan under Taliban rule, where girls were forbidden from attending school. Despite facing death threats and violence, Malala continued to advocate for girls' education, speaking out against the injustices she witnessed in her community. In 2012, Malala was shot in the head by a member of the Taliban, but miraculously survived and continued her activism. Her story gained international attention, leading to her being awarded the Nobel Peace Prize in 2014. Malala's courage and resilience in the face of unimaginable obstacles serve as a powerful reminder of the importance of standing up for what you believe in, even in the face of adversity. These real-life examples of individuals who have overcome adversity serve as a source of inspiration and motivation for anyone facing challenges in their own lives. Whether it be Oprah Winfrey's rise from poverty to success, J. K. Rowling's journey from rejection to literary fame, or Malala Yousafzai's fight for girls' education in the face of danger, these individuals demonstrate the power of resilience, perseverance, and belief in oneself. So, the next time you find yourself facing obstacles, remember these stories and draw strength from their examples. With hard work, determination, and a positive attitude, you too can overcome any obstacle that stands in your way.

Chapter 8: Self-Reflection and Self-Care

- Importance of self-reflection in personal growth

Self-reflection is a crucial component of personal growth and development. It is a process of pausing to think about our thoughts, emotions, and actions in order to gain a deeper understanding of ourselves and our experiences. By taking the time to reflect on our daily interactions, decisions, and behaviors, we can learn about our strengths and areas for improvement. Self-reflection allows us to become more self-aware, which is essential for personal growth.

One of the key benefits of self-reflection is that it helps us to identify and understand our emotions. By examining our feelings and the reasons behind them, we can gain insight into our reactions to certain situations. This awareness enables us to manage our emotions more effectively and develop emotional intelligence. When we are able to recognize and regulate our emotions, we can improve our relationships with others and make better decisions. Self-reflection also allows us to recognize patterns in our emotions, which can help us to address any underlying issues that may be causing distress.

Self-reflection is also important for gaining a deeper understanding of our values, beliefs, and goals. By taking the time to reflect on what is truly important to us, we can align our actions with our core values and beliefs. This alignment leads to a sense of purpose and fulfillment in life. Additionally, self-reflection helps us to set and achieve meaningful goals. By evaluating our progress and identifying areas for improvement, we can make adjustments to our plans and stay focused on our objectives. Self-reflection encourages us to take ownership of our lives and make intentional choices that align with our values and goals.

Another important aspect of self-reflection is that it fosters personal growth and development. By reflecting on our experiences and learning from them, we can adapt and grow as individuals. Self-reflection allows us to recognize our strengths and build on them, as well as identify areas for improvement and work on them. This continuous process of self-improvement is essential for personal growth and development. Through self-reflection, we can learn from our mistakes, celebrate our successes, and evolve into the best version of ourselves.

In addition to fostering personal growth, self-reflection also enhances critical thinking skills. By analyzing our thoughts, emotions, and actions, we can develop a deeper understanding of ourselves and the world around us. This analytical mindset enables us to evaluate situations from different perspectives and make informed decisions. Critical thinking skills are essential for success in both personal and professional life, as they help us to solve problems, communicate effectively, and navigate complex situations. Self-reflection can also improve our ability to learn from our experiences and adapt to new challenges.

Self-reflection is a practice that can be cultivated through various methods, such as journaling, meditation, and mindful awareness. By incorporating self-reflection into our daily routine, we can develop a habit of introspection that will support our personal growth and development. It is important to approach self-reflection with an open mind and a willingness to learn about ourselves. By being honest and non-judgmental in our reflections, we can gain valuable insights that will help us to grow and thrive. Self-reflection is a powerful tool for personal growth, and by making it a priority in our lives, we can unlock our full potential and become the best version of ourselves.

- Practices for self-care and maintaining well-being

In today's fast-paced and demanding world, it is increasingly important to prioritize self-care and well-being. Taking care of ourselves mentally, physically, and emotionally is essential for overall health and happiness. There are numerous practices that can help us achieve this balance and maintain a sense of well-being. By incorporating these practices into our daily routines, we can better cope with the stressors of life and improve our overall quality of life.

One of the key practices for self-care and well-being is maintaining a healthy lifestyle. This includes eating a balanced diet, getting regular exercise, and getting plenty of rest. Eating a variety of fruits and vegetables, whole grains, and lean protein can help fuel our bodies and minds. Regular exercise, such as walking, running, or yoga, can help reduce stress and improve mood. Getting an adequate amount of sleep each night is also important for overall health and well-being. By taking care of our bodies through these practices, we can better cope with the challenges of everyday life.

Another important practice for self-care and well-being is setting boundaries and saying no when necessary. It is important to prioritize our own needs and not overextend ourselves. Learning to say no to commitments that do not align with our values or goals can help reduce stress and prevent burnout. Setting boundaries with others in our personal and professional lives can also help protect our mental and emotional well-being. By honoring our own needs and boundaries, we can take better care of ourselves and maintain a sense of balance in our lives.

Practicing mindfulness and meditation is another effective way to promote self-care and well-being. Mindfulness involves being fully present in the moment and paying attention to our thoughts and feelings without judgment. This practice can help reduce stress, improve focus, and enhance overall well-being. Meditation, which involves quieting the mind and focusing on the breath, can also help calm the nervous system and promote relaxation. By incorporating mindfulness and meditation into our daily routines, we can cultivate a sense of inner peace and resilience that can help us navigate life's challenges with grace and ease.

Building and maintaining strong social connections is also crucial for self-care and well-being. Humans are social beings and thrive on connection with others. Spending time with friends and loved ones, sharing experiences, and offering support can help boost mood and improve overall well-being. Joining clubs, organizations, or support groups can also provide opportunities for social connection and a sense of belonging. By nurturing our relationships and building a support network, we can feel more connected, valued, and supported in our lives.

Lastly, practicing self-compassion and self-acceptance is an important component of self-care and well-being. It is important to treat ourselves with kindness and understanding, especially when facing challenges or setbacks. By cultivating self-compassion, we can learn to be more forgiving of ourselves and embrace our imperfections. Practicing self-acceptance involves acknowledging and embracing all aspects of ourselves, including our strengths and weaknesses. By practicing self-compassion and self-acceptance, we can cultivate a sense of inner peace and well-being that can help us navigate life's ups and downs with grace and resilience. By taking care of ourselves mentally, physically, emotionally, and socially, we can better cope with the stressors of life and improve our quality of life. By focusing on maintaining a healthy lifestyle, setting boundaries, practicing mindfulness and meditation, building strong social connections, and cultivating self-compassion and self-acceptance, we can promote self-care and well-being in our lives. By prioritizing our own needs and well-being, we can live more fulfilling and balanced lives.

- Balancing self-improvement with self-compassion

Self-improvement and self-compassion are two important aspects of personal growth and development. However, finding the balance between these two can be challenging for many individuals. On one hand, self-improvement involves setting goals, pushing ourselves to be better, and working towards personal growth. On the other hand, self-compassion involves being kind and understanding towards ourselves, accepting our flaws and mistakes, and treating ourselves with the same empathy and respect that we would show to a friend.

One way to strike a balance between self-improvement and self-compassion is to practice self-awareness. This means being mindful of our thoughts, emotions, and actions, and recognizing when we are being too hard on ourselves or overly critical. By developing a greater sense of self-awareness, we can learn to identify when we need to push ourselves to improve and when we need to be kind and compassionate towards ourselves.

Another important aspect of balancing self-improvement with self-compassion is setting realistic and achievable goals. While it is important to challenge ourselves and strive for growth, it is also important to set goals that are realistic and attainable. Setting unrealistic goals can lead to feelings of failure and inadequacy, which can erode our self-esteem and undermine our self-compassion. By setting goals that are challenging yet achievable, we can push ourselves to grow without setting ourselves up for disappointment and self-criticism.

It is also important to practice self-compassion when we experience setbacks or failures in our pursuit of self-improvement. Failure is a natural part of the learning process, and it is important to treat ourselves with kindness and understanding when things do not go as planned. Instead of beating ourselves up or dwelling on our mistakes, we can practice self-compassion by acknowledging our efforts, learning from our failures, and moving forward with a sense of resilience and determination.

In addition to self-awareness and goal-setting, cultivating self-compassion involves practicing self-care and self-acceptance. This means taking care of our physical, emotional, and mental well-being, and treating ourselves with the same care and respect that we would show to others. Self-care activities such as exercise, meditation, and spending time with loved ones can help us recharge and rejuvenate, while self-acceptance involves acknowledging and embracing our strengths and weaknesses, and recognizing that we are worthy of love and compassion just as we are.

To terminate, it is important to remember that self-improvement and self-compassion are not mutually exclusive concepts, but rather complementary aspects of personal growth and development. By finding a balance between pushing ourselves to grow and accepting ourselves with kindness and compassion, we can achieve a greater sense of well-being and fulfillment in our lives. By practicing self-awareness, setting realistic goals, treating ourselves with kindness and understanding, and cultivating self-care and self-acceptance, we can strike a healthy balance between self-improvement and self-compassion and lead happier, more fulfilling lives.

Chapter 9: Perseverance and Persistence

- The role of perseverance in achieving success

Perseverance is a crucial trait that plays a significant role in achieving success in various aspects of life. Whether it be in academic pursuits, career advancement, personal goals, or overcoming obstacles, the ability to persevere through challenges and setbacks is essential for reaching one's full potential. The dictionary defines perseverance as the steadfastness in doing something despite difficulty or delay in achieving success. This definition highlights the importance of resilience and determination in achieving one's goals. It is through perseverance that individuals are able to push through obstacles, setbacks, and failures, and ultimately achieve success.

Success is often not a linear path, but rather a series of ups and downs, obstacles, and challenges. It is those who are able to persevere through these difficulties who ultimately reach their goals and achieve success. Perseverance is what sets successful individuals apart from those who give up when faced with adversity. It is the ability to keep going, to keep trying, even when things seem impossible or overwhelming. Without perseverance, it is easy to become discouraged, lose motivation, and ultimately give up on our goals. However, with perseverance, we are able to stay focused, determined, and committed to achieving success.

Research has shown that perseverance is a key predictor of success in various fields, including education, business, sports, and personal development. Individuals who exhibit perseverance are more likely to overcome obstacles, learn from their mistakes, and ultimately achieve their goals. In academia, for example, students who persevere through difficult courses, exams, and assignments are more likely to succeed in their studies and achieve high grades. Similarly, in business, entrepreneurs who persevere through challenges, rejections, and failures are more likely to build successful businesses and achieve their financial goals.

One of the key benefits of perseverance is that it builds resilience and determination. When we persevere through challenges and setbacks, we develop the mental strength and fortitude to keep going, even when things seem difficult. This resilience allows us to bounce back from failures, setbacks, and disappointments, and continue working towards our goals. It is through perseverance that we build the determination and grit necessary to overcome obstacles and achieve success. Without perseverance, it is easy to become discouraged, lose motivation, and give up on our goals. However, with perseverance, we are able to stay focused, determined, and committed to achieving success.

Perseverance also helps us develop a growth mindset, which is the belief that our abilities and intelligence can be developed through hard work, effort, and perseverance. Individuals with a growth mindset are more likely to take on challenges, learn from their mistakes, and ultimately achieve success. This is because they view setbacks and failures as opportunities for growth and improvement, rather than as signs of inadequacy or incompetence. By persevering through challenges and setbacks, we are able to cultivate a growth mindset and develop the belief that we are capable of achieving our goals through hard work and determination.

In addition to building resilience and a growth mindset, perseverance also helps us stay focused and committed to our goals. When we persevere through challenges and setbacks, we develop the ability to stay focused on our long-term objectives and not get distracted by short-term setbacks or failures. This focus allows us to keep our eye on the prize and continue working towards our goals, even when things seem difficult or overwhelming. By staying committed to our goals and persevering through challenges, we increase our chances of achieving success and reaching our full potential. It is through perseverance that individuals are able to push through obstacles, setbacks, and failures, and ultimately reach their goals. Perseverance builds resilience, determination, and a growth mindset, which are essential qualities for achieving success. By staying focused, committed, and determined, individuals can overcome challenges, learn from their mistakes, and ultimately achieve their goals.

- Strategies for cultivating persistence

Persistence is a key trait that contributes significantly to the success of individuals in various aspects of life, including academics, careers, and personal endeavors. It involves the ability to stay focused on goals despite challenges and setbacks, to persevere through difficulties, and to continue striving towards achievement. Cultivating persistence requires deliberate effort and the implementation of effective strategies to overcome obstacles and maintain motivation over the long term.

One of the fundamental strategies for cultivating persistence is setting clear and achievable goals. When individuals have a clear understanding of what they want to achieve, they are more likely to stay committed to their efforts and persevere through challenges. Breaking down larger goals into smaller, more manageable tasks can also help individuals maintain motivation and momentum as they work towards their objectives. Additionally, setting deadlines and creating a plan of action can provide a sense of structure and direction, helping to prevent procrastination and maintain a sense of progress.

Another important strategy for cultivating persistence is developing a growth mindset. Individuals with a growth mindset believe that their abilities can be improved through hard work and effort, rather than viewing them as fixed traits. This mindset allows individuals to see setbacks and failures as opportunities for growth and learning, rather than as insurmountable obstacles. By reframing challenges as opportunities to develop new skills and improve performance, individuals can maintain motivation and resilience in the face of difficulties.

Building a strong support network is also crucial for cultivating persistence. Surrounding oneself with friends, family, mentors, or colleagues who provide encouragement, support, and guidance can help individuals stay motivated and focused on their goals. Supportive relationships can also provide accountability and motivation, as individuals are more likely to persevere when they know that others are rooting for their success. Additionally, seeking out role models who have demonstrated persistence and resilience can inspire individuals to stay committed to their goals and overcome challenges.

Practicing self-care and maintaining a healthy work-life balance are essential for cultivating persistence. Taking care of one's physical, emotional, and mental well-being can help individuals stay motivated and resilient in the face of challenges. Regular exercise, proper nutrition, adequate sleep, and stress-management techniques can all contribute to increased energy levels, focus, and resilience. Additionally, engaging in activities outside of work or school that bring joy and fulfillment can help individuals recharge and maintain a sense of perspective and balance.

In closing, celebrating small wins and milestones along the way is an important strategy for cultivating persistence. Recognizing and rewarding progress, no matter how small, can help individuals stay motivated and maintain momentum towards their goals. Whether it's treating oneself to a small indulgence, sharing achievements with friends and family, or simply reflecting on how far one has come, celebrating successes can provide a boost of motivation and reaffirm individuals' commitment to their goals. By acknowledging and appreciating the progress made, individuals can build confidence and resilience to continue persevering through challenges and setbacks. Setting clear and achievable goals, developing a growth mindset, building a strong support network, practicing self-care, and celebrating small wins along the way are all essential components of cultivating persistence. By implementing these strategies and fostering a determined attitude towards achieving one's objectives, individuals can develop the resilience and determination needed to overcome challenges and achieve success in their endeavors.

- Stories of individuals who have persevered against all odds

Perseverance is a quality that is often admired in individuals who face difficult circumstances. Throughout history, there have been countless stories of individuals who have demonstrated incredible resilience in the face of adversity. These stories serve as a source of inspiration for others, showing that it is possible to overcome seemingly insurmountable obstacles with determination and perseverance.

One such individual is Malala Yousafzai, a Pakistani activist for female education and the youngest Nobel Prize laureate. Malala's story is one of incredible courage and determination in the face of extreme adversity. At the age of 15, she was shot in the head by a Taliban gunman while on her way home from school. Despite the grave nature of her injuries, Malala refused to be silenced. She continued to speak out for the rights of girls to receive an education, even at great personal risk. Her resilience and perseverance have made her a global symbol of the power of education and the importance of standing up for one's beliefs.

Another remarkable story of perseverance is that of Nelson Mandela, the South African anti-apartheid revolutionary and political leader who served as President of South Africa from 1994 to 1999. Mandela spent 27 years in prison for his activism against the apartheid regime, during which time he endured harsh conditions and brutal treatment. Despite the immense challenges he faced, Mandela never lost sight of his goal of a free and democratic South Africa. Upon his release from prison, he continued to fight for justice and reconciliation, ultimately leading his country to a peaceful transition to democracy. Mandela's story is a testament to the power of perseverance in the face of injustice and oppression.

In the realm of literature, the story of J.K. Rowling serves as an inspiring example of perseverance in the face of failure. Before finding success with the Harry Potter series, Rowling faced countless rejections from publishers and financial struggles as a single mother. Despite these setbacks, she never gave up on her dream of becoming a published author. Rowling's perseverance paid off when the first book in the Harry Potter series was finally published in 1997, becoming a worldwide phenomenon. Her story is a reminder that success often requires perseverance in the face of failure and rejection.

The story of Nick Vujicic, an Australian motivational speaker born with a rare disorder called Tetra-amelia syndrome, is another inspiring example of perseverance against all odds. Vujicic was born without limbs, facing immense physical and emotional challenges from a young age. Despite the obstacles he faced, Vujicic refused to let his disability define his life. He went on to become a successful motivational speaker, inspiring millions of people around the world with his message of hope and resilience. Vujicic's story serves as a powerful reminder that one's circumstances do not have to dictate their future, and that with perseverance and determination, anything is possible.

These stories, and many others like them, serve as a testament to the power of perseverance in the face of adversity. They remind us that no matter how difficult our circumstances may be, we have the ability to overcome challenges and achieve our goals. By drawing inspiration from these individuals who have persevered against all odds, we can find the strength and determination to face our own struggles with courage and resilience. Their stories serve as a beacon of hope and a reminder that with perseverance, anything is possible.

Chapter 10: Adaptability and Flexibility

- Importance of being adaptable in a changing world

In today's rapidly changing world, the ability to adapt is becoming increasingly important. As technology advances and global markets evolve, individuals and organizations must be able to quickly adjust to new circumstances in order to stay competitive and achieve success. Being adaptable means being able to respond effectively to change and uncertainty, while also being open to new ideas and ways of doing things. This flexibility is essential for navigating the complexities of the modern world and is a key attribute that can set individuals and organizations apart from their peers.

One of the main reasons why adaptability is so crucial in today's world is the pace of change. Technology is advancing at an unprecedented rate, and the ways in which we live and work are constantly being transformed. In order to keep up with these changes, individuals must be willing to constantly learn and grow, and be willing to adapt their skills and perspectives as needed. Those who are able to embrace change and adapt quickly will be better positioned to take advantage of new opportunities and navigate the challenges that come with constant evolution.

Another reason why adaptability is important is the increasing interconnectedness of the global economy. In today's world, businesses must compete on a global scale, and the ability to adapt to different cultures, markets, and ways of doing business is essential for success. Those who are able to embrace diversity and adapt to new environments will be better able to build relationships, negotiate effectively, and thrive in a rapidly changing marketplace. Similarly, individuals who are able to adapt to different work styles and expectations will be more likely to succeed in a world where collaboration and teamwork are increasingly important.

Furthermore, adaptability is important in a changing world because it allows individuals and organizations to remain resilient in the face of uncertainty.

The ability to quickly assess new situations, make decisions, and take action is essential for thriving in times of crisis or upheaval. Those who are able to adapt in the face of adversity will be better able to weather challenges and emerge stronger on the other side. By being adaptable, individuals and organizations can turn challenges into opportunities and continue to grow and prosper even in the face of uncertainty.

In addition to these reasons, adaptability is important in a changing world because it enables individuals and organizations to innovate and stay ahead of the curve. By being open to new ideas and ways of doing things, individuals can continuously improve and evolve, leading to greater creativity and productivity. Similarly, organizations that are able to adapt quickly to new technologies and market trends will be better positioned to innovate and develop new products and services that meet the needs of an ever-changing world. In this way, adaptability is not just important for surviving in a changing world, but also for thriving and leading the pack. By being open to change, willing to learn, and able to respond effectively to new situations, individuals and organizations can stay competitive and achieve success. In a world where technology is advancing rapidly, the global economy is increasingly interconnected, and uncertainty is a constant, adaptability is the key to thriving and growing. By embracing change, being open to new ideas, and remaining resilient in the face of challenges, individuals and organizations can position themselves for success in an ever-evolving world. Ultimately, adaptability is not just a valuable skill to have, but a necessary one for navigating the complexities of the modern world and achieving long-term success.

- Techniques for embracing change and flexibility

Change is an inevitable and constant aspect of life, and in today's fast-paced world, the ability to adapt and be flexible is more crucial than ever. Embracing change and flexibility requires a proactive mindset and the willingness to let go of old ways of thinking and doing things. By adopting certain techniques, individuals can navigate through periods of change with grace and resilience, ultimately thriving in the face of uncertainty.

One key technique for embracing change is to cultivate a growth mindset. This mindset, as described by psychologist Carol Dweck, is characterized by the belief that one's abilities and intelligence can be developed through hard work and dedication. Individuals with a growth mindset are more open to learning and trying new things, and are less likely to be discouraged by setbacks. By fostering a growth mindset, individuals can approach change as an opportunity for personal and professional growth, rather than as a threat.

Another important technique for embracing change is to practice mindfulness. Mindfulness involves being fully present in the moment and non-judgmentally observing one's thoughts and emotions. By cultivating mindfulness, individuals can become more aware of their reactions to change and better equipped to respond thoughtfully and rationally. Mindfulness can also help individuals manage stress and anxiety that often accompany periods of change, allowing them to navigate through uncertainty with clarity and composure.

In addition to cultivating a growth mindset and practicing mindfulness, developing a strong support network is crucial for embracing change. Surrounding oneself with supportive and understanding individuals can provide a sense of security and encouragement during times of transition. Friends, family, colleagues, mentors, and coaches can offer valuable perspective, feedback, and emotional support, helping individuals navigate through challenges and emerge stronger on the other side. Building and maintaining strong relationships is essential for fostering resilience and adaptability in the face of change.

Furthermore, setting clear goals and priorities can help individuals navigate through periods of change with purpose and direction. By identifying what is most important and relevant in their personal and professional lives, individuals can make informed decisions and take intentional actions that align with their values and aspirations. Setting realistic and achievable goals can provide a sense of clarity and motivation, guiding individuals through uncertainty and helping them stay focused on what truly matters.

Lastly, embracing change involves embracing the unknown and being open to new possibilities. Change often brings about uncertainty and ambiguity, which can be uncomfortable and challenging for many individuals. By reframing uncertainty as an opportunity for growth and exploration, individuals can approach change with a sense of curiosity and excitement, rather than fear and resistance. Embracing the unknown requires a willingness to step outside of one's comfort zone, take risks, and embrace new experiences and perspectives. By embracing change with an open mind and heart, individuals can unlock new opportunities for personal and professional growth, and ultimately thrive in the face of uncertainty. By cultivating a growth mindset, practicing mindfulness, building a strong support network, setting clear goals and priorities, and embracing the unknown, individuals can approach change with grace, resilience, and adaptability. By embracing change as an opportunity for growth and exploration, individuals can navigate through uncertainty with confidence and emerge stronger and more resilient on the other side.

- Examples of successful people who have thrived by being adaptable

Flexibility and adaptability are crucial traits for success in today's rapidly changing world. Many successful individuals have demonstrated the power of being adaptable in various fields, showing how they have thrived by being able to adjust to new circumstances and challenges. One example of a successful person who exemplifies adaptability is Elon Musk. As the CEO of Tesla and SpaceX, Musk has faced numerous setbacks and obstacles in his career but has always found a way to pivot and adapt to overcome them. His ability to quickly change course and find creative solutions has enabled him to achieve incredible success in the technology and space industries.

Another example of a successful individual who has thrived by being adaptable is Oprah Winfrey. From humble beginnings, Winfrey has gone on to become one of the most influential media moguls in the world. Throughout her career, she has faced challenges and setbacks but has always been able to adapt and evolve. Whether it was transitioning from television to launching her own successful network, OWN, or expanding her brand into various industries, Winfrey has shown the power of adaptability in achieving success.

In the world of sports, Serena Williams is a prime example of an athlete who has thrived by being adaptable. Throughout her career, Williams has faced injuries, setbacks, and fierce competition, but she has always found a way to adapt her game and continue to dominate the tennis world. Whether it was adjusting her training regimen, changing her playing style, or overcoming mental hurdles, Williams has consistently demonstrated the power of adaptability in achieving success on the court.

In the business world, Jeff Bezos is another example of a successful individual who has thrived by being adaptable. As the founder and CEO of Amazon, Bezos has navigated the rapidly changing landscape of e-commerce and technology by constantly adapting and evolving his business strategies. From expanding into new markets to introducing innovative technologies, Bezos has shown how adaptability is crucial for success in the fast-paced world of business. By being able to pivot, adjust, and innovate in the face of challenges, these individuals have been able to overcome obstacles and achieve their goals. In today's constantly evolving world, adaptability is a key trait that can set individuals apart and help them succeed in their endeavors. Whether in technology, media, sports, or business, the ability to adapt is crucial for achieving success and thriving in any field.

Chapter 11: Resilience in the Face of Failure

- How to bounce back from failure

Failure is an inevitable part of life, and the way we handle setbacks can greatly impact our future success. When faced with failure, it is important to remember that it does not define who we are as individuals. Instead, it is an opportunity for growth and learning. By approaching failure with a positive mindset, we can turn a negative experience into a valuable lesson.

One of the first steps to bouncing back from failure is to accept the reality of the situation. It can be tempting to deny or ignore our failures, but this only prolongs the healing process and prevents us from moving forward. By acknowledging our mistakes and taking responsibility for them, we can begin to learn from our failures and make positive changes in the future.

It is also important to resist the urge to dwell on past mistakes. While it is natural to feel upset or disappointed after a failure, ruminating on what went wrong can lead to feelings of self-doubt and insecurity. Instead, focus on what can be learned from the experience and how to improve in the future. By shifting our perspective from one of self-criticism to self-reflection, we can use failure as a stepping stone to success.

Another key aspect of bouncing back from failure is to seek support from others. Surrounding ourselves with a supportive network of friends, family, and mentors can provide valuable perspective and encouragement during challenging times. When we share our failures and struggles with others, we can gain new insights, feedback, and advice that can help us navigate difficult situations more effectively.

In addition to seeking support from others, it is important to practice self-care during times of failure. This may involve engaging in activities that promote relaxation and emotional well-being, such as exercise, meditation, or spending time with loved ones. Taking care of ourselves physically and emotionally can help us regain perspective and build resilience in the face of setbacks.

To summarize, it is crucial to maintain a growth mindset when bouncing back from failure. Instead of viewing failure as a permanent and insurmountable obstacle, see it as an opportunity for growth and development. By approaching failure with a growth mindset, we can harness the lessons learned from setbacks to propel us forward and achieve greater success in the future. By accepting the reality of the situation, reframing our perspective, seeking support, practicing self-care, and maintaining a growth mindset, we can turn failures into valuable learning experiences that propel us closer to our goals. Remember, failure is not the end of the road - it is simply a detour on the journey to success.

- Learning from setbacks and mistakes

Learning from setbacks and mistakes is an essential part of personal and professional growth. When we encounter obstacles or make errors, it can be easy to become discouraged or frustrated. However, by reframing these challenges as opportunities for learning and improvement, we can turn setbacks into stepping stones towards success.

One of the key ways to learn from setbacks and mistakes is to reflect on what went wrong and why. This involves taking a step back from the situation and critically evaluating the factors that contributed to the setback. By examining our actions, decisions, and thought processes, we can better understand what went awry and identify areas for improvement. This process of self-reflection requires honesty and humility, as it may reveal uncomfortable truths about our own shortcomings or mistakes. However, by confronting these truths head-on, we can begin the process of learning and growth.

Another important aspect of learning from setbacks and mistakes is to seek feedback from others. Often, we may be too close to a situation to see it objectively, or we may lack the perspective to fully grasp the implications of our actions. By seeking feedback from colleagues, mentors, or friends, we can gain valuable insights and perspectives that can help us better understand what went wrong and how to avoid similar mistakes in the future. Constructive criticism can be difficult to hear, but it is essential for growth and development.

In addition to reflection and feedback, it is important to take action to address the root causes of setbacks and mistakes. This may involve making changes to our behavior, processes, or strategies to prevent similar errors from occurring in the future. It may also involve seeking out new skills or knowledge to better equip ourselves for future challenges. By taking proactive steps to address the underlying issues that led to the setback, we can not only learn from our mistakes but also ensure that we are better prepared for future challenges.

It is also important to adopt a growth mindset when learning from setbacks and mistakes. Rather than viewing setbacks as permanent failures or a reflection of our abilities, we should see them as opportunities for growth and development. By approaching setbacks with a growth mindset, we can maintain a positive attitude and a sense of resilience in the face of challenges. This can help us bounce back from setbacks more quickly and effectively, and ultimately lead to greater success in the long run.

In brief, it is important to practice self-compassion when dealing with setbacks and mistakes. It is natural to feel disappointment, frustration, or even shame when things go wrong. However, it is important to remember that setbacks and mistakes are a normal part of the learning process, and that everyone makes errors from time to time. By practicing self-compassion and treating ourselves with kindness and understanding, we can more easily bounce back from setbacks and move forward with confidence and resilience. By reflecting on what went wrong, seeking feedback from others, taking proactive action, adopting a growth mindset, and practicing self-compassion, we can turn setbacks into opportunities for learning and improvement. By embracing setbacks as valuable learning experiences, we can become better equipped to handle future challenges and ultimately achieve greater success in our personal and professional lives.

- Encouraging stories of individuals who have turned failure into success

Failure is a natural part of life, and it's something that everyone experiences at one point or another. However, what truly sets individuals apart is how they are able to turn their failures into successes. Through perseverance, determination, and a positive mindset, many individuals have been able to overcome setbacks and achieve their goals. These stories of triumph in the face of adversity serve as a source of inspiration and motivation for others who may be struggling with their own failures.

One such inspiring story is that of J.K. Rowling, the author of the Harry Potter series. Rowling faced numerous rejections from publishers before finally finding success. She was living on welfare and struggling to make ends meet while working on the first book in the series. Despite the setbacks and challenges she faced, Rowling never gave up on her dream of becoming a published author. Her persistence paid off when Harry Potter and the Sorcerer's Stone was finally published, launching her to literary stardom. Rowling's story is a powerful reminder that failure is not the end, but rather a stepping stone to success.

Another notable example is that of Michael Jordan, widely regarded as one of the greatest basketball players of all time. Jordan was cut from his high school basketball team, a devastating blow for any aspiring athlete. However, instead of letting this setback discourage him, Jordan used it as motivation to work harder and prove his doubters wrong. His dedication and work ethic paid off, as he went on to win six NBA championships and earn numerous accolades throughout his career. Jordan's story serves as a testament to the power of perseverance and determination in the face of failure.

In the world of business, Steve Jobs is often cited as a prime example of turning failure into success. Jobs was famously ousted from Apple, the company he co-founded, only to return years later and lead it to unprecedented success. His journey was marked by numerous setbacks and failures, but Jobs never lost sight of his vision and passion for innovation. Through his resilience and determination, he was able to transform Apple into one of the most valuable and influential companies in the world. Jobs' story is a testament to the importance of staying true to one's goals and never giving up, even in the face of adversity.

These stories of individuals who have turned failure into success serve as a powerful reminder that setbacks are not the end of the road, but rather an opportunity for growth and transformation. By embracing failure as a learning experience and using it as motivation to push forward, individuals can achieve great things and surpass even their own expectations. As these inspiring examples have shown, success is not defined by the absence of failure, but rather by the ability to rise above it and emerge stronger than before. So the next time you face a setback or stumble on your journey towards your goals, remember these stories and let them inspire you to keep pushing forward, no matter what obstacles may come your way.

Chapter 12: The Power of Positive Thinking

- The impact of positive thinking on success

Positive thinking is a powerful mindset that has been shown to have a significant impact on an individual's success. Research has demonstrated that individuals who maintain a positive outlook are more likely to achieve their goals, overcome obstacles, and experience higher levels of overall well-being. This is due to the fact that positive thinking can lead to increased motivation, resilience, and a greater sense of self-efficacy. By approaching challenges with a positive mindset, individuals are better able to adapt to change, remain focused on their goals, and persevere in the face of adversity.

One of the key ways in which positive thinking influences success is by enabling individuals to maintain a growth mindset. A growth mindset is the belief that one's abilities and intelligence can be developed through effort, learning, and perseverance. This mindset is essential for success because it fosters a willingness to take on challenges, learn from mistakes, and continuously improve. By maintaining a positive outlook, individuals are more likely to embrace challenges as opportunities for growth rather than viewing them as insurmountable obstacles. This mindset empowers individuals to take risks, push themselves out of their comfort zones, and continue to strive for excellence.

Furthermore, positive thinking has been shown to have a direct impact on an individual's physical and mental well-being. Research has demonstrated that individuals who maintain a positive outlook are less likely to experience stress, anxiety, and depression. This is because positive thinking can help individuals cope with difficult situations, regulate their emotions, and maintain a sense of perspective. By cultivating a positive mindset, individuals are better equipped to handle the ups and downs of life, maintain a sense of balance, and focus on the things that truly matter. This in turn can lead to increased levels of happiness, satisfaction, and overall well-being.

In addition to the personal benefits of positive thinking, research has also shown that individuals who maintain a positive outlook are more likely to be successful in their professional lives. This is because positive thinking can lead to increased levels of creativity, innovation, and problem-solving abilities. By approaching challenges with a positive mindset, individuals are better able to think outside the box, come up with novel solutions, and adapt to changing circumstances. This can be especially important in today's rapidly evolving business landscape, where the ability to innovate and adapt is critical for success.

Moreover, positive thinking can also have a profound impact on an individual's relationships and social connections. Research has shown that individuals who maintain a positive outlook are more likely to have strong social support networks, healthy relationships, and a greater sense of connectedness. This is because positive thinking can lead to a more optimistic and empathetic outlook, which can in turn foster positive interactions with others. By approaching social situations with a positive mindset, individuals are more likely to build meaningful connections, resolve conflicts constructively, and maintain strong relationships with others. By maintaining a positive outlook, individuals can cultivate a growth mindset, enhance their physical and mental well-being, improve their professional performance, and strengthen their relationships. This is because positive thinking has the ability to boost motivation, resilience, and self-efficacy, leading to greater levels of achievement, happiness, and fulfillment. As such, cultivating a positive mindset is an essential skill for success in all areas of life.

- Techniques for cultivating a positive mindset

Having a positive mindset is essential for success and overall well-being. Cultivating a positive mindset involves developing a mindset that is focused on optimism, gratitude, and resilience. It involves training yourself to see the good in every situation, no matter how challenging it may be. This mindset can greatly impact your mental health, relationships, and overall quality of life. In this article, we will explore some techniques for cultivating a positive mindset and how you can incorporate them into your daily life.

One of the first steps in cultivating a positive mindset is practicing gratitude. Gratitude involves being thankful for the good things in your life, no matter how big or small. It can help you shift your focus from what is lacking to what you have, which can help boost your mood and overall outlook on life. One way to practice gratitude is to keep a gratitude journal. Each day, take a few minutes to write down three things that you are grateful for. This can help you cultivate a habit of focusing on the positive aspects of your life, rather than dwelling on the negatives.

Another technique for cultivating a positive mindset is to practice positive self-talk. The way you speak to yourself can greatly impact your mindset and self-esteem. Instead of being critical or self-deprecating, try to speak to yourself in a kind and encouraging manner. Replace negative thoughts with positive affirmations, such as "I am capable," "I am resilient," or "I am worthy of love and happiness. " By practicing positive self-talk, you can train your mind to focus on the good in yourself and in others.

Mindfulness is another powerful technique for cultivating a positive mindset. Mindfulness involves paying attention to the present moment without judgment. It can help you become more aware of your thoughts and emotions, which can help you better understand and manage them. By practicing mindfulness, you can train your mind to focus on the present moment rather than worrying about the past or future. You can practice mindfulness through activities such as meditation, deep breathing, or simply taking a few minutes each day to focus on your breath and observe your thoughts without judgment.

In addition to gratitude, positive self-talk, and mindfulness, practicing self-care is also essential for cultivating a positive mindset. Self-care involves taking care of your physical, emotional, and mental well-being. This can include getting enough sleep, eating nutritious foods, exercising regularly, and engaging in activities that bring you joy and relaxation. By taking care of yourself, you can better cope with stress and challenges, which can help you maintain a positive mindset.

Building resilience is another important technique for cultivating a positive mindset. Resilience involves bouncing back from setbacks and challenges, and learning from them. It involves developing coping skills and strategies that can help you navigate difficult situations with grace and optimism. One way to build resilience is to practice self-compassion. Instead of being hard on yourself when things don't go as planned, try to treat yourself with kindness and understanding. By building resilience, you can develop a positive mindset that can help you overcome obstacles and thrive in the face of adversity. By practicing gratitude, positive self-talk, mindfulness, self-care, and resilience, you can train your mind to focus on the good in every situation. These techniques can help you develop a mindset that is optimistic, resilient, and grateful, which can greatly impact your mental health and overall quality of life. By incorporating these techniques into your daily routine, you can cultivate a positive mindset that can help you thrive in all areas of your life.

- Examples of individuals who attribute their success to positive thinking

Positive thinking is a powerful tool that can help individuals achieve success in various aspects of their lives. Countless successful people have attributed their achievements to the power of positive thinking. One such individual is Oprah Winfrey, who is widely regarded as one of the most successful and influential figures in the world. Oprah has often spoken about how positive thinking has played a crucial role in her success. She believes that having a positive mindset has helped her overcome challenges and obstacles, and has allowed her to achieve her goals and dreams.

Another example of an individual who attributes their success to positive thinking is Richard Branson, the founder of the Virgin Group. Branson is known for his optimistic attitude and belief in the power of positive thinking. He has stated that maintaining a positive mindset has been essential to his success as an entrepreneur. Branson believes that having a positive outlook on life has enabled him to take risks, persevere through failures, and achieve incredible success in business.

In addition to Oprah Winfrey and Richard Branson, there are many other successful individuals who credit their achievements to positive thinking. One such example is Tony Robbins, a renowned motivational speaker and life coach.

Robbins has inspired millions of people around the world to adopt a positive mindset and take control of their lives. He believes that positive thinking is the key to unlocking one's full potential and achieving success in all areas of life.

Furthermore, athletes are also known for using positive thinking to achieve success. Michael Jordan, considered one of the greatest basketball players of all time, often spoke about the importance of maintaining a positive attitude on and off the court. Jordan believed that having a positive mindset was crucial to his success as a basketball player, and he used positive affirmations and visualization techniques to stay focused and motivated. Whether it be Oprah Winfrey, Richard Branson, Tony Robbins, Michael Jordan, or countless other successful individuals, the power of positive thinking has been a common thread among those who have achieved greatness. By adopting a positive mindset, setting goals, and believing in oneself, anyone can overcome challenges, achieve their dreams, and reach their full potential. So, let us all embrace the power of positive thinking and strive for success in all areas of our lives.

Chapter 13: Networking and Building a Support System

- Importance of networking for success

Networking is a critical component of success in today's competitive business world. It involves building relationships with other professionals in your industry, as well as potential clients or customers. By networking effectively, you can open up new opportunities, gather valuable information, and build a strong support system that can help you navigate the challenges of a fast-paced and ever-changing marketplace.

One of the key reasons why networking is so important for success is that it allows you to tap into a wealth of knowledge and expertise that can help you grow and develop as a professional. By connecting with other individuals who have experience and insight in your field, you can learn from their successes and failures, gain new perspectives on your own work, and expand your skill set in ways that can open up new opportunities for advancement.

Networking also provides you with access to valuable resources and contacts that can help you achieve your goals. Whether you're looking to land a new job, secure a new client, or find a mentor who can help guide you through the next stage of your career, having a strong network of contacts can make all the difference. By cultivating relationships with key players in your industry, you can stay informed about the latest trends and developments, access new opportunities for growth and collaboration, and build a strong foundation for long-term success.

Another important benefit of networking is that it can help you build your personal brand and establish yourself as a thought leader in your field. By sharing your knowledge and expertise with others, participating in industry events and conferences, and engaging in online discussions and forums, you can raise your profile and increase your credibility among your peers. This can lead to new opportunities for speaking engagements, media appearances, and other forms of professional recognition that can help you stand out in a crowded marketplace.

In addition to the tangible benefits of networking, there are also numerous intangible benefits that can help you achieve greater success in your career. By connecting with other professionals who share your passion and drive, you can find inspiration, motivation, and support to help you stay focused and committed to your goals. Networking can also provide you with a sense of belonging and community that can help you feel more connected and engaged in your work, leading to greater job satisfaction and overall well-being.

While building a strong network of contacts takes time and effort, the rewards are well worth the investment. By actively seeking out opportunities to connect with other professionals, participating in industry events, and staying engaged in online networking platforms, you can cultivate a strong and diverse network that can help you achieve your goals and overcome the obstacles that stand in your way. By harnessing the power of networking, you can create a solid foundation for success that will serve you well throughout your career.

- Building a strong support system

Building a strong support system is essential for personal growth and well-being. Having a network of people who can provide emotional support, guidance, and encouragement can help individuals navigate life's challenges more effectively. Whether it's friends, family members, mentors, or colleagues, a strong support system can provide a sense of belonging and connection that is crucial for mental and emotional health.

One of the key components of building a strong support system is surrounding yourself with people who share your values and goals. When you have a support system of like-minded individuals, you are more likely to feel understood and validated. This can create a sense of camaraderie and mutual respect that can be incredibly empowering. By surrounding yourself with people who share your values, you can build a strong foundation of trust and understanding that will hold you up during difficult times.

Another important aspect of building a strong support system is being willing to give as well as receive support. Building relationships is a two-way street, and it's important to be there for others in their time of need as well. By offering support to others, you not only strengthen your relationships but also create a sense of reciprocity that can enhance your own sense of well-being. By being a supportive presence in the lives of others, you can cultivate a sense of community and connection that is deeply fulfilling.

In addition to surrounding yourself with like-minded individuals and offering support to others, it's important to be willing to ask for help when you need it. Building a strong support system means being vulnerable and open to receiving help from others. It's okay to lean on your support system when you're feeling overwhelmed or struggling to cope with a challenging situation. By reaching out for help when you need it, you are showing that you value and trust the people in your support system, and you are allowing them to be there for you in your time of need.

Another important aspect of building a strong support system is setting boundaries. While it's important to be open and vulnerable with your support system, it's also important to maintain healthy boundaries in your relationships. Boundaries are essential for maintaining your own well-being and ensuring that your relationships are mutually respectful and supportive. By setting boundaries with your support system, you can ensure that your needs are being met and that you are not overextending yourself in your relationships.

Communication is another key element of building a strong support system. It's important to communicate openly and honestly with the people in your support system about your needs, concerns, and emotions. By expressing yourself authentically, you can deepen your connections with others and create a sense of trust and understanding that is essential for a strong support system. Effective communication can help you navigate conflicts and misunderstandings, and can foster a sense of mutual respect and empathy that can strengthen your relationships. By surrounding yourself with like-minded individuals, offering support to others, being willing to ask for help, setting boundaries, and communicating effectively, you can create a network of people who will uplift and empower you in your journey through life. A strong support system can provide a sense of belonging, connection, and community that is vital for mental and emotional health. By investing time and energy into building and nurturing your support system, you can create a foundation of resilience and strength that will carry you through life's challenges with grace and courage.

- Tips for effective networking and relationship-building

Networking and relationship-building are crucial skills for success in both professional and personal life. Building a strong network of connections can open doors to new opportunities, help you gather valuable advice and support, and ultimately aid in advancing your career. Whether you are a seasoned professional or just starting out in your career, there are several key tips to keep in mind to ensure effective networking and relationship-building.

First and foremost, it is important to approach networking with a genuine and authentic mindset. Building relationships based on trust and mutual respect is essential for long-term success. Take the time to understand the needs and interests of your connections, and offer your support and assistance whenever possible. Remember that networking is about building lasting relationships, not just accumulating a list of contacts.

Another important tip for effective networking is to be proactive in seeking out opportunities to connect with others. Attend industry events, conferences, and networking mixers to meet new people and expand your professional network. Additionally, utilize online networking platforms such as LinkedIn to connect with professionals in your field and stay updated on industry trends and news. Networking requires effort and initiative, so be prepared to put yourself out there and make meaningful connections.

In addition to being proactive in your networking efforts, it is also important to be strategic in your approach. Identify key individuals who you would like to connect with and research their background and interests before reaching out to them. Make a plan for how you will engage with these contacts and follow up after initial interactions to maintain the relationship. Remember that networking is a two-way street, so be prepared to offer value to your connections in return for their time and assistance.

Building strong relationships takes time and effort, so it is important to be patient and persistent in your networking efforts. Be consistent in your communication with your contacts, whether through regular emails, phone calls, or in-person meetings. Remember that relationships are built on trust and reliability, so demonstrate your commitment to your connections by staying in touch and offering your support whenever needed.

Lastly, don't forget to leverage your existing relationships to expand your network even further. Ask your contacts for introductions to their connections who may be beneficial for you to connect with. Don't be afraid to ask for help or advice from your network when needed, as most people are willing to offer support to those they trust and respect. By utilizing your existing relationships to build new connections, you can expand your network exponentially and create a strong support system for your career growth. By approaching networking with authenticity, proactivity, and strategy, you can build strong relationships that will support your career growth and open doors to new opportunities. Remember to be patient and persistent in your networking efforts, and leverage your existing relationships to expand your network even further. With these tips in mind, you can build a strong network of connections that will help you succeed in your career and beyond.

Chapter 14: Financial Literacy and Wealth Management

- Understanding financial principles for success

In order to achieve success in the realm of finance, it is essential to have a deep understanding of financial principles. These principles serve as the foundation for making sound financial decisions, managing investments wisely, and creating a secure financial future. By comprehending these principles, individuals and businesses can navigate the complexities of the financial landscape with confidence and competence.

One of the key financial principles that is crucial for success is the concept of budgeting. Budgeting involves creating a plan for how to allocate financial resources in order to achieve specific goals. By establishing a budget, individuals and businesses can track their income and expenses, identify areas where spending can be reduced, and prioritize financial objectives. Budgeting is a fundamental tool for ensuring that financial resources are used efficiently and effectively, and it is an essential practice for achieving financial success.

Another important financial principle for success is the concept of saving and investing. Saving involves setting aside a portion of income for future use, while investing involves putting money into assets with the expectation of generating a return. By saving and investing wisely, individuals and businesses can build wealth over time, protect against financial emergencies, and achieve long-term financial goals. Understanding the different types of investments, the risks and rewards associated with each, and the importance of diversification is essential for success in the realm of finance.

Risk management is another critical financial principle that is essential for success. Risk management involves identifying, assessing, and mitigating potential risks that could impact financial stability and success. By understanding the various types of risks that exist in the financial world, such as market risk, credit risk, and operational risk, individuals and businesses can develop strategies for managing these risks effectively. Implementing risk management practices can help protect financial assets, prevent financial losses, and ensure long-term financial success.

A final financial principle that is essential for success is the concept of financial literacy. Financial literacy involves having the knowledge and skills to understand basic financial concepts, make informed financial decisions, and effectively manage financial resources. By improving financial literacy, individuals and businesses can increase their ability to navigate the complexities of the financial world, make sound financial choices, and achieve financial success. Investing in financial education, seeking out professional advice, and staying informed about financial trends and developments are all key strategies for enhancing financial literacy and ultimately achieving success in the realm of finance. By embracing concepts such as budgeting, saving and investing, risk management, and financial literacy, individuals and businesses can build a solid foundation for achieving financial goals, managing financial resources effectively, and creating a secure financial future. By mastering these principles and incorporating them into daily financial practices, individuals and businesses can increase their financial acumen, make informed financial decisions, and ultimately achieve long-term financial success.

- Strategies for managing and growing wealth

Managing and growing wealth is a crucial aspect of financial success and stability. Individuals who are able to effectively manage their wealth not only secure their financial future but also have the opportunity to grow their assets for long-term success. There are various strategies that can be employed to manage and grow wealth, from diversifying investment portfolios to developing a sound savings plan. By understanding these strategies and implementing them effectively, individuals can take control of their financial well-being and work towards achieving their financial goals.

One key strategy for managing and growing wealth is diversification. Diversification involves spreading investments across a range of assets, such as stocks, bonds, real estate, and commodities, to reduce risk and maximize returns. By diversifying their investment portfolio, individuals can protect themselves against market fluctuations and potential losses in any one asset class. This not only helps to safeguard their wealth but also allows for potential growth through different sources of income.

Another important strategy for managing and growing wealth is developing a sound savings plan. Saving money is a fundamental aspect of wealth management and is essential for building a solid financial foundation. By setting aside a portion of income for savings, individuals can create a safety net for emergencies, future expenses, and investment opportunities. It is recommended that individuals aim to save at least 10-15% of their income on a regular basis to ensure financial security and growth.

In addition to diversification and saving, investing wisely is also a key strategy for managing and growing wealth. Investing in assets that have the potential for long-term growth and income can help individuals build and expand their wealth over time. This may include investing in stocks, mutual funds, real estate, or starting a business. It is important for individuals to conduct thorough research and seek professional advice before making investment decisions to ensure that they align with their financial goals and risk tolerance.

Moreover, staying informed and educated about financial markets and trends is essential for managing and growing wealth. By staying up-to-date on market conditions, economic indicators, and investment opportunities, individuals can make informed decisions that can lead to better financial outcomes. This may involve reading financial news, attending seminars or workshops, or consulting with a financial advisor. Keeping abreast of financial information can help individuals identify opportunities for growth and navigate potential risks.

Furthermore, practicing sound financial habits, such as living within one's means, avoiding excessive debt, and maintaining a budget, is also crucial for managing and growing wealth. By practicing discipline and restraint in spending, individuals can free up resources for savings and investments, which can ultimately lead to wealth accumulation. Developing financial literacy and understanding concepts such as interest rates, inflation, and compounding can also help individuals make better financial decisions and maximize their wealth potential. By implementing these strategies effectively and consistently, individuals can take control of their financial future, protect their assets, and work towards achieving their financial goals. With careful planning, discipline, and a long-term perspective, individuals can build wealth, secure their financial well-being, and create a legacy for future generations.

- Stories of individuals who have achieved financial success

Financial success is something that many individuals aspire to achieve in their lives. Whether it be through hard work, dedication, or sheer luck, there are countless stories of people who have achieved financial success through various means. These success stories serve as inspiration to others who may be on their own journey towards financial stability and independence.

One such story is that of Elon Musk, the founder of Tesla and SpaceX. Musk has built a vast empire of companies and has amassed a fortune worth billions of dollars. His journey to success was not without its challenges, as he faced numerous setbacks along the way. However, Musk's perseverance, determination, and innovative thinking ultimately led to his success. His story serves as an example of how hard work, creativity, and resilience can lead to financial success.

Another individual who has achieved financial success is Oprah Winfrey. Winfrey is a media mogul, talk show host, and philanthropist who has built a media empire worth billions of dollars. Despite facing numerous obstacles in her life, including poverty and abuse, Winfrey rose above her circumstances to become one of the most successful and influential women in the world. Her story is a testament to the power of resilience, determination, and self-belief in achieving financial success.

Warren Buffett is another individual who has achieved immense financial success through his career as an investor and businessman. Buffett is widely regarded as one of the most successful and savvy investors in the world, with a net worth of billions of dollars. His investment strategies and philosophies have been studied and emulated by countless individuals seeking to achieve financial success. Buffett's story is a testament to the power of smart investing, patience, and long-term thinking in building wealth and achieving financial success.

These stories of individuals who have achieved financial success serve as inspiration and motivation for others on their own journeys towards financial independence. While the paths to financial success may vary, these individuals share common traits such as perseverance, determination, creativity, and a strong work ethic. By studying and learning from their stories, aspiring entrepreneurs and investors can gain valuable insights and guidance on how to navigate the challenges and obstacles on the road to financial success. These success stories demonstrate the power of hard work, determination, resilience, and innovative thinking in overcoming obstacles and achieving success. By studying and learning from the experiences of these successful individuals, aspiring entrepreneurs and investors can gain valuable insights and guidance on how to navigate the challenges and pitfalls on their own journeys towards financial success. Ultimately, the key to financial success lies in believing in oneself, staying focused on one's goals, and never giving up on the pursuit of one's dreams.

Chapter 15: Health and Wellness Practices

- Importance of prioritizing physical and mental health

Physical and mental health are two vital aspects of overall well-being that greatly impact our daily lives. While both are interconnected and deeply intertwined, they are often treated as separate entities in our society. However, it is crucial to prioritize both physical and mental health equally, as neglecting one can have detrimental effects on the other. By maintaining a balance between the two, individuals can achieve optimal health and lead fulfilling lives.

Physical health encompasses the body's overall well-being, including factors such as fitness, nutrition, and sleep. It is essential to engage in regular physical activity, eat a balanced diet, and get an adequate amount of rest in order to maintain good physical health. Physical activity not only helps to improve cardiovascular health and strengthen muscles but also plays a critical role in regulating mood and reducing stress. A nutritious diet rich in vitamins, minerals, and antioxidants nourishes the body and supports its various functions. Additionally, getting enough quality sleep is essential for rejuvenating the body and mind, as lack of sleep can lead to a host of health issues, including cognitive impairment and decreased immune function.

Similarly, mental health is just as important as physical health and refers to the state of one's emotional, psychological, and social well-being. It is crucial to take care of our mental health by practicing self-care, managing stress, and seeking help when needed. Self-care activities, such as meditation, mindfulness, and journaling, can help to promote emotional well-being and reduce anxiety and depression. Managing stress through relaxation techniques, such as deep breathing exercises and yoga, can also significantly impact mental health by reducing the body's stress response and promoting a sense of inner calm. It is important to remember that seeking help from a mental health professional is not a sign of weakness but a courageous step towards improving one's mental well-being.

The connection between physical and mental health is undeniable, as they both influence each other in profound ways. For example, regular exercise has been shown to have numerous mental health benefits, such as reducing symptoms of anxiety and depression. Exercise increases the production of endorphins, neurotransmitters that act as natural painkillers and mood elevators, leading to a greater sense of well-being. Furthermore, physical activity can help to improve self-esteem and body image, leading to a more positive outlook on life. On the other hand, poor physical health, such as chronic illnesses or injuries, can also have a significant impact on mental well-being, leading to feelings of isolation, frustration, and helplessness.

Conversely, mental health issues, such as stress, anxiety, and depression, can also manifest in physical symptoms, such as headaches, muscle tension, and digestive problems. Chronic stress, in particular, can have a debilitating impact on the body, leading to an increased risk of cardiovascular disease, obesity, and diabetes. It is crucial to address mental health concerns in a timely manner in order to prevent the development of physical health issues. By prioritizing both physical and mental health, individuals can achieve a state of overall well-being and resilience to life's challenges. By taking care of our bodies through regular physical activity, proper nutrition, and adequate rest, we can support our overall health and vitality. Additionally, by practicing self-care, managing stress, and seeking help when needed, we can nurture our mental well-being and promote emotional resilience. It is important to remember that physical and mental health are deeply interconnected and influence each other in profound ways. By prioritizing both aspects of health equally, we can achieve a state of balance and harmony that promotes a healthy and happy life.

- Tips for maintaining a healthy lifestyle

Maintaining a healthy lifestyle is crucial for overall well-being and longevity. There are several key tips that can help individuals achieve and sustain a healthy lifestyle. One of the most important tips is to prioritize physical activity. Regular exercise has numerous benefits, including improved cardiovascular health, weight management, and mood regulation. It is recommended that adults engage in at least 150 minutes of moderate-intensity exercise per week, such as brisk walking, cycling, or swimming.

In addition to physical activity, it is essential to maintain a balanced diet. A healthy diet should include a variety of fruits, vegetables, whole grains, lean proteins, and healthy fats. Avoiding processed foods, sugary drinks, and excessive amounts of salt and saturated fats is also important. Drinking plenty of water throughout the day is another key component of a healthy diet. Staying hydrated helps to maintain energy levels, regulate body temperature, and aid in digestion.

Another tip for maintaining a healthy lifestyle is to prioritize sleep. Getting an adequate amount of quality sleep is essential for cognitive function, mood regulation, and overall health. Most adults need between 7-9 hours of sleep per night to function optimally. Establishing a regular sleep schedule and creating a relaxing bedtime routine can help improve sleep quality.

Stress management is also crucial for maintaining a healthy lifestyle. Chronic stress can have negative effects on both physical and mental health. Finding healthy ways to cope with stress, such as practicing mindfulness, deep breathing, or engaging in relaxing activities like yoga or meditation, can help reduce the impact of stress on the body. It is important to recognize when stress levels are high and take steps to manage and reduce stress before it has a negative impact on health.

In addition to physical activity, diet, sleep, and stress management, maintaining social connections is also important for overall health and well-being. Strong social connections can provide emotional support, reduce feelings of loneliness and isolation, and improve mental health. Making time for friends and family, joining social groups or clubs, or volunteering in the community are all ways to nurture social connections and improve overall well-being.

Consistency is key when it comes to maintaining a healthy lifestyle. Making small, sustainable changes over time can lead to long-term success. Setting realistic goals, tracking progress, and celebrating achievements along the way can help individuals stay motivated and committed to a healthy lifestyle. It is important to approach health and wellness as a journey rather than a destination, and to be kind and patient with oneself throughout the process. By prioritizing these key areas and making small, sustainable changes over time, individuals can improve their overall health and well-being. Remember that it is never too late to start making positive changes for better health, and that consistency and dedication are key to long-term success. With the right mindset and support system in place, anyone can achieve and maintain a healthy lifestyle.

- Examples of successful individuals who prioritize their health

Prioritizing health is a key factor in achieving success in all aspects of life. It is essential to understand that one cannot reach their full potential if they neglect their well-being. There are countless examples of successful individuals who have made their health a priority and have reaped the benefits in their personal and professional lives.

One such example is Oprah Winfrey, a media mogul and philanthropist who has been open about her struggles with weight and health in the past. After years of yo-yo dieting and fluctuating weight, Winfrey made a conscious decision to prioritize her health by embracing a balanced diet and regular exercise routine. By making small, sustainable changes to her lifestyle, Winfrey was able to not only lose weight but also improve her overall health and well-being. This commitment to self-care has undoubtedly contributed to her continued success in the world of media and beyond.

Another notable example is Richard Branson, the billionaire entrepreneur behind the Virgin Group. Branson is known for his adventurous spirit and bold business ventures, but he also recognizes the importance of taking care of his health. Despite his busy schedule and demanding work commitments, Branson prioritizes his physical fitness by engaging in various activities such as kiteboarding, tennis, and cycling. By staying active and maintaining a healthy lifestyle, Branson is able to sustain his energy levels and mental acuity, enabling him to lead his company to new heights of success.

In the world of sports, Serena Williams is a prime example of an athlete who prioritizes her health to excel in her career. As one of the greatest tennis players of all time, Williams understands the importance of maintaining peak physical condition to compete at the highest level. She follows a rigorous training regimen, incorporates healthy eating habits, and ensures she gets enough rest and recovery to prevent injuries and stay at the top of her game. Williams' dedication to her health has not only led to numerous Grand Slam titles but also serves as an inspiration to aspiring athletes worldwide.

In the field of technology, Tim Cook, the CEO of Apple Inc., is a shining example of a successful individual who places a high value on his health. Cook has been vocal about his commitment to fitness and mindfulness practices, such as cycling and meditation, which help him stay grounded amid the demands of running a tech giant. By making time for self-care and prioritizing his well-being, Cook is able to lead Apple with clarity and focus, driving the company's innovation and growth.

These examples underscore the importance of prioritizing health in achieving success. Whether in the realms of media, business, sports, or technology, individuals who make their health a priority are better equipped to handle the challenges and pressures that come with success. By taking care of their physical, mental, and emotional well-being, they are able to perform at their best, make sound decisions, and maintain a balanced and fulfilling life. Ultimately, prioritizing health is not just about achieving success but also about living a vibrant and meaningful life.

Chapter 16: Leadership and Influence

- Qualities of effective leaders

Leadership is a complex and multi-faceted concept that has intrigued scholars and practitioners for centuries. Effective leaders possess a unique set of qualities that enable them to guide and inspire their followers towards achieving common goals. These qualities are essential for success in any organization, whether it be in the corporate world, politics, education, or any other field. In this essay, we will explore the key qualities of effective leaders and how they can be cultivated and developed.

One of the most important qualities of effective leaders is vision. A visionary leader has a clear sense of direction and purpose, and is able to articulate this vision to others in a compelling and inspiring way. This clarity of vision enables the leader to set goals and objectives that are aligned with the organization's mission and values, and to guide their followers towards achieving them. Visionary leaders are able to see the big picture, anticipate future trends and challenges, and develop strategies to address them. They are able to inspire others to share in their vision and work towards a common goal.

Another essential quality of effective leaders is integrity. Integrity is the foundation of trust, and without trust, a leader cannot effectively lead their followers. Leaders with integrity are honest, ethical, and transparent in their actions and decisions. They do what they say they will do, and they hold themselves and others accountable to the highest ethical standards. Integrity builds credibility and respect, and it is essential for building strong relationships with followers and other stakeholders. Leaders with integrity are consistent in their words and actions, and they are reliable and trustworthy.

Empathy is another key quality of effective leaders. Empathy is the ability to understand and share the feelings and perspectives of others, and it is essential for building strong relationships and fostering collaboration and teamwork. Leaders who are empathetic are able to connect with their followers on a personal level, and they are able to inspire trust, loyalty, and respect. Empathetic leaders are able to listen actively and attentively to others, and they are able to understand the needs, concerns, and aspirations of their followers. They are able to create a supportive and inclusive environment where everyone feels valued and respected.

Effective communication is another essential quality of effective leaders. Communication is the foundation of leadership, and without effective communication, a leader cannot effectively convey their vision, goals, and expectations to their followers. Leaders who are strong communicators are able to articulate their ideas clearly and concisely, and they are able to adapt their communication style to the needs and preferences of their audience. They are able to listen actively and attentively to others, and they are able to provide feedback and guidance in a constructive and supportive manner. Effective communicators are able to inspire, motivate, and influence others, and they are able to build strong relationships based on trust and respect.

Adaptability is another key quality of effective leaders. In today's fast-changing and unpredictable world, leaders must be able to adapt to new challenges and opportunities, and to lead their followers through times of uncertainty and change. Leaders who are adaptable are open-minded, flexible, and resilient, and they are able to navigate complex and ambiguous situations with ease. They are able to embrace change, learn from their mistakes, and continuously improve and innovate. Adaptable leaders are able to inspire confidence and trust in their followers, and they are able to lead by example in times of crisis and uncertainty. These qualities include vision, integrity, empathy, effective communication, and adaptability. Developing these qualities requires self-awareness, continuous learning, and a commitment to personal and professional growth. Effective leaders are able to create a positive and inclusive work environment where everyone feels valued and respected, and where collaboration and teamwork thrive. By cultivating these qualities and leading with purpose and passion, leaders can make a positive impact on their organizations, their followers, and society as a whole.

- Techniques for influencing others

Influencing others is a key aspect of interpersonal communication, leadership, and management. It involves the ability to persuade and convince others to change their attitudes, beliefs, or behaviors. There are several techniques that can be used to effectively influence others, ranging from persuasion and negotiation to emotional intelligence and assertiveness.

One of the most common techniques for influencing others is persuasion. This involves presenting a convincing argument or case for why a particular course of action should be taken. Persuasion relies on logic, reasoning, and evidence to sway others to your point of view. It is important to tailor your argument to the needs and interests of the person you are trying to influence. This could involve highlighting the benefits of a particular decision, addressing any potential objections or concerns, and demonstrating how it aligns with their goals and values.

Another effective technique for influencing others is negotiation. Negotiation involves a give-and-take process where both parties work towards a mutually beneficial outcome. This could involve compromising, finding common ground, or exploring creative solutions to reach a consensus. Effective negotiation skills are essential for influencing others in a collaborative and constructive way. It is important to listen actively, communicate clearly, and be open to feedback and alternative perspectives.

Emotional intelligence is another key factor in influencing others. Emotional intelligence involves the ability to recognize and manage your own emotions, as well as understand and empathize with the emotions of others. By being aware of your own emotions and how they impact your behavior, you can better regulate your responses and communicate effectively with others. This can help build trust, rapport, and credibility, which are essential for influencing others in a positive and constructive way.

Assertiveness is another important technique for influencing others. Assertiveness involves expressing your opinions, needs, and boundaries in a confident and respectful manner. It is about standing up for yourself and advocating for what you believe in, without being aggressive or passive. Assertive communication involves being clear, direct, and honest in expressing your views, while also being open to feedback and alternative perspectives. By being assertive, you can build credibility, establish boundaries, and influence others in a respectful and effective way. By using techniques such as persuasion, negotiation, emotional intelligence, and assertiveness, you can effectively sway others to your point of view and achieve your goals. It is important to tailor your approach to the needs and interests of the person you are trying to influence, while also being open to feedback and alternative perspectives. By developing your influencing skills, you can build trust, credibility, and rapport with others, and achieve success in your personal and professional relationships.

- Case studies of successful leaders and their strategies

Leadership is a crucial aspect of organizational success and plays a pivotal role in shaping the trajectory of a company. Throughout history, there have been numerous examples of successful leaders who have deftly navigated challenges and steered their organizations towards growth and prosperity. By examining the case studies of these leaders and their strategies, we can gain valuable insights into the qualities and approaches that contribute to effective leadership.

One such example is the case of Steve Jobs, the co-founder and former CEO of Apple Inc. Known for his visionary approach and innovative ideas, Jobs was able to transform Apple into one of the most valuable companies in the world. His leadership style was characterized by a relentless pursuit of excellence and a keen focus on design and user experience. Jobs was not afraid to take risks and was known for his willingness to push the boundaries of what was possible. His ability to anticipate market trends and create products that captured the imagination of consumers set Apple apart from its competitors.

Another leader worth examining is Indra Nooyi, the former CEO of PepsiCo. Nooyi is widely regarded as one of the most successful female executives in the world and is known for her strategic acumen and leadership skills. During her tenure at PepsiCo, she implemented a number of initiatives that helped the company outperform its competitors and achieve significant growth. Nooyi's leadership style emphasized the importance of diversity and inclusivity, and she was a vocal advocate for social responsibility and sustainability. Under her guidance, PepsiCo launched several successful products and expanded its presence in emerging markets.

The case of Jeff Bezos, the founder and CEO of Amazon, also provides valuable insights into effective leadership strategies. Bezos is known for his relentless focus on customer satisfaction and his willingness to disrupt traditional business models in pursuit of growth. His leadership style is characterized by a strong emphasis on innovation and a commitment to long-term thinking. Bezos has built Amazon into one of the world's largest and most successful companies by continually reinventing the customer experience and investing in new technologies. His ability to anticipate market trends and his relentless pursuit of operational excellence have been key drivers of Amazon's success.

One common thread among these successful leaders is their ability to inspire and motivate their teams. Effective leaders understand the importance of building a strong organizational culture and creating an environment where employees feel empowered and motivated to achieve their best. By setting clear goals and expectations, providing mentorship and support, and recognizing and rewarding achievement, leaders can create a positive work environment that fosters collaboration and innovation.

In addition to inspiring their teams, successful leaders also demonstrate strong decision-making skills. By analyzing data, considering multiple perspectives, and weighing the potential risks and rewards of different options, leaders can make informed decisions that support the long-term goals of the organization. Effective leaders are not afraid to make tough choices or challenge the status quo, but they do so with a clear understanding of the potential implications and a willingness to take responsibility for their decisions. From visionary leaders like Steve Jobs to strategic thinkers like Indra Nooyi to disruptors like Jeff Bezos, there are numerous examples of leaders who have navigated challenges and achieved success through their leadership skills. By understanding the key characteristics and strategies that have enabled these leaders to excel, we can learn valuable lessons that can be applied in our own leadership roles. Ultimately, effective leadership is a combination of inspiration, decision-making, and strategic thinking, and by emulating the approaches of successful leaders, we can enhance our own leadership capabilities and drive success in our organizations.

Chapter 17: Giving Back and Making a Difference

- Importance of giving back to the community

Giving back to the community is a fundamental aspect of being a responsible and engaged member of society. By actively contributing to the well-being of those around us, we not only enrich the lives of others but also cultivate a sense of purpose and fulfillment within ourselves. In today's fast-paced and interconnected world, the importance of giving back to the community cannot be overstated. Whether through volunteering, charitable donations, or simply lending a helping hand to those in need, there are countless ways in which we can make a positive impact on the world around us.

One of the key benefits of giving back to the community is the sense of connection and belonging that it fosters. When we reach out to others in need, we forge meaningful relationships and establish a sense of solidarity with those around us. This sense of community is crucial for building strong and resilient societies, as it allows individuals to come together to support each other in times of need. By giving back to the community, we not only strengthen our personal connections with others but also contribute to the overall well-being and cohesion of the society as a whole.

Furthermore, giving back to the community is a powerful way to create positive change and address social issues. Whether it's helping to feed the homeless, volunteering at a local school, or supporting a nonprofit organization, every act of giving has the potential to make a real difference in the lives of others. By actively engaging with the needs of our community, we can help to alleviate suffering, promote equality, and create a more just and compassionate world for all. Through our collective efforts, we can work towards building a society where everyone has the opportunity to thrive and succeed.

In addition to its social impact, giving back to the community also has numerous personal benefits. Research has shown that individuals who engage in acts of kindness and generosity are more likely to experience greater levels of happiness, satisfaction, and well-being. By giving back to others, we not only improve the lives of those around us but also cultivate a sense of gratitude, empathy, and compassion within ourselves. These positive feelings can have a ripple effect, leading to increased feelings of connection, purpose, and fulfillment in our own lives.

Moreover, giving back to the community can also help to develop important skills and qualities that are valuable in both personal and professional contexts. Through volunteering, for example, individuals can gain valuable experience in leadership, teamwork, communication, and problem-solving. These skills can be particularly useful in the workplace, where employers increasingly value candidates who demonstrate a commitment to social responsibility and community engagement. By giving back to the community, we not only enrich our own lives but also enhance our professional opportunities and prospects for success. By reaching out to others in need, we can create stronger connections, address social issues, promote positive change, and cultivate personal growth and fulfillment. Whether through volunteering, charitable donations, or acts of kindness, there are countless ways in which we can contribute to the well-being of our community and make a difference in the lives of others. By embracing the importance of giving back, we can help to create a more compassionate, inclusive, and thriving society for all.

- How to make a positive impact in the world

Making a positive impact in the world is a goal that many people aspire to achieve. Whether it be through acts of kindness, charitable donations, volunteering, or advocating for important social issues, there are countless ways to make a difference in the lives of others and contribute to a better world. In this essay, we will explore various strategies and approaches for making a positive impact, as well as the importance of making a conscious effort to do so.

One of the most effective ways to make a positive impact in the world is through acts of kindness and compassion. Simple gestures such as offering a helping hand to someone in need, listening attentively to a friend who is going through a difficult time, or showing empathy and understanding towards others can go a long way in brightening someone's day and making a positive difference in their life. Kindness is a universal language that transcends barriers and brings people together, fostering a sense of connection and community that is essential for creating a harmonious and supportive society.

Another powerful way to make a positive impact in the world is through charitable donations and philanthropy. By supporting organizations and causes that are dedicated to addressing pressing social issues such as poverty, hunger, healthcare, education, and environmental conservation, individuals can make a tangible difference in the lives of those who are less fortunate and contribute to the greater good of society as a whole. Making a financial contribution to a reputable charity or nonprofit organization can help fund essential programs and services that improve the well-being and quality of life for marginalized and vulnerable populations.

Volunteering is another meaningful way to make a positive impact in the world. By dedicating your time and skills to serve others in need, you can make a direct and immediate impact on the lives of individuals and communities. There are countless opportunities for volunteering in various fields such as healthcare, education, social services, environmental conservation, and animal welfare, allowing you to find a cause that aligns with your interests and values. Volunteering not only benefits those in need but also provides a sense of fulfillment, purpose, and personal growth for the volunteer.

Advocating for important social issues is also a crucial way to make a positive impact in the world. By raising awareness, speaking out against injustice, and fighting for equality and human rights, individuals can bring about meaningful change and create a more inclusive and equitable society for all. Whether it be through participating in peaceful protests, signing petitions, writing to elected officials, or engaging in dialogue with others, advocacy is a powerful tool for driving social progress and promoting positive social change. It is important to educate yourself on key issues, amplify the voices of marginalized communities, and use your platform and privilege to advocate for those who are often silenced or marginalized. By practicing kindness, supporting charitable organizations, volunteering, and advocating for important social issues, we can each contribute to a better world and make a lasting difference in the lives of others. It is important to remember that even small acts of kindness and generosity can have a ripple effect and inspire others to do the same, creating a positive cycle of giving and compassion that benefits us all. Let us continue to strive for a world where empathy, compassion, and solidarity are the guiding principles that shape our interactions and relationships with one another. Together, we can build a brighter future for generations to come.

- Examples of successful individuals who have used their success to help others

Success is often measured by personal achievements, wealth, and fame. However, there are individuals who have used their success as a platform to make a positive impact on the lives of others. These individuals have dedicated their time, resources, and influence to support causes that are close to their hearts and make a difference in the world. By using their success to help others, they have not only changed lives but have also inspired others to do the same.

One such example of a successful individual who uses her success to help others is Oprah Winfrey. As one of the most influential television personalities in the world, Oprah has dedicated her platform to promoting education, empowering women, and supporting various charitable causes. Through her media empire, she has raised awareness about important issues, such as childhood education, poverty, and women's rights. In addition, Oprah has established the Oprah Winfrey Leadership Academy for Girls in South Africa, which provides education and support to disadvantaged young women. By using her success and influence, Oprah has made a significant impact on the lives of many individuals and inspired others to give back to their communities.

Another example of a successful individual who has used his success to help others is Bill Gates. As the co-founder of Microsoft and one of the wealthiest individuals in the world, Bill Gates has dedicated a large portion of his wealth to philanthropic efforts through the Bill and Melinda Gates Foundation. The foundation focuses on improving global health, eradicating poverty, and promoting education around the world. By investing in research and development, providing grants to community organizations, and supporting various initiatives, Bill Gates has made a significant impact on global health and education. Through his foundation, he has also inspired other wealthy individuals to give back and make a difference in the world.

One more example of a successful individual who has used his success to help others is Warren Buffett. As one of the most successful investors in the world, Warren Buffett has pledged to give away the majority of his wealth to charitable causes through the Giving Pledge initiative. Through his charitable contributions, Buffett has supported various causes, such as education, healthcare, and poverty alleviation. By using his success and wealth to help others, Buffett has made a significant impact on the lives of many individuals and has inspired other wealthy individuals to give back to their communities. Through their dedication, generosity, and commitment to making a difference, these individuals have made a positive impact on the lives of many individuals and have inspired others to do the same. By using their success as a platform for good, they have shown that success is not just about personal achievements but also about making a difference in the world. As we continue to strive for success in our own lives, let us remember the importance of using our success to help others and make a positive impact on the world around us.

Chapter 18: Conclusion

- Recap of key habits for success

Success is often seen as the ultimate goal in both personal and professional endeavors. However, the path to success is not always clear and can be filled with obstacles and challenges. In order to achieve success, it is essential to develop key habits that are conducive to growth and progress. These habits are not only beneficial for achieving success, but also for maintaining it over the long term.

One of the most important habits for success is goal setting. Setting clear, specific, and achievable goals provides a roadmap for success and helps to keep you focused and motivated. In order to set effective goals, it is important to establish both short-term and long-term objectives that are measurable and attainable. By regularly reviewing and reassessing your goals, you can track your progress and make any necessary adjustments to stay on track.

Another key habit for success is time management. Time is a finite resource, and how you choose to allocate it can greatly impact your level of success. Effective time management involves prioritizing tasks, setting deadlines, and avoiding procrastination. By creating a schedule and sticking to it, you can maximize your productivity and ensure that you are using your time wisely. Additionally, setting aside time for self-care and relaxation is crucial for maintaining a healthy work-life balance and preventing burnout.

Communication skills are also essential for success. Whether in a professional or personal context, the ability to communicate effectively is crucial for building relationships, resolving conflicts, and achieving your goals. Good communication involves active listening, clear and concise expression of ideas, and the ability to adapt your communication style to different situations and audiences. By honing your communication skills, you can effectively convey your ideas, build strong relationships, and collaborate more effectively with others.

Adaptability is another key habit for success. In today's fast-paced and constantly changing world, the ability to adapt to new circumstances and challenges is essential for staying relevant and competitive. By being open to new ideas, willing to learn new skills, and flexible in your approach, you can better navigate the uncertainties and complexities of modern life. Embracing change and seeing it as an opportunity for growth and innovation can help you stay ahead of the curve and seize new opportunities as they arise.

Lastly, resilience is a crucial habit for success. Facing setbacks and failures is inevitable on the path to success, but it is how you respond to these challenges that ultimately determines your level of success. Resilience involves the ability to bounce back from adversity, learn from your mistakes, and persevere in the face of obstacles. By cultivating a positive mindset, self-belief, and a willingness to keep pushing forward despite setbacks, you can overcome any hurdles that come your way and ultimately achieve your goals. By setting goals, managing your time effectively, honing your communication skills, adapting to change, and cultivating resilience, you can position yourself for success in both your personal and professional life. These habits are not only beneficial for achieving success, but also for sustaining it over the long term. By incorporating these habits into your daily routine and making them a priority, you can set yourself up for a lifetime of success and fulfillment.

- Encouragement to continue cultivating these habits

In today's fast-paced world, it can be easy to lose sight of the importance of cultivating good habits. However, taking the time to establish and maintain positive habits can have a profound impact on our personal and professional lives. By consistently engaging in behaviors that support our well-being and growth, we can enhance our overall quality of life and achieve our goals more effectively.

One key habit that is worth cultivating is setting specific and achievable goals. Having clear goals provides direction and motivation, and helps us stay focused on what is most important to us. By taking the time to define what we want to achieve and breaking it down into smaller, actionable steps, we increase our chances of successfully reaching our desired outcomes. Regularly reviewing and adjusting our goals as needed allows us to stay on track and make progress towards our aspirations.

Another important habit to cultivate is practicing self-care. Taking care of ourselves physically, mentally, and emotionally is essential for maintaining our well-being and resilience. This can include activities such as getting regular exercise, eating a balanced diet, getting enough sleep, and engaging in activities that bring us joy and relaxation. By prioritizing our self-care, we can reduce stress, improve our mood, and enhance our overall quality of life.

In addition to setting goals and practicing self-care, it is also beneficial to cultivate the habit of continuous learning and growth. In today's rapidly changing world, staying current and expanding our knowledge and skills is essential for keeping up with the demands of work and life. Engaging in lifelong learning through reading, taking courses, attending workshops, and seeking out new experiences can help us adapt to new challenges, seize opportunities, and expand our horizons.

Furthermore, cultivating the habit of gratitude can have a profound impact on our well-being and happiness. Taking the time to acknowledge and appreciate the blessings in our lives, both big and small, can increase our overall sense of fulfillment and satisfaction. By regularly practicing gratitude through journaling, mindfulness, or simply expressing thanks to others, we can cultivate a more positive outlook and foster stronger relationships with those around us. By setting specific goals, practicing self-care, engaging in continuous learning, and cultivating gratitude, we can enhance our quality of life and achieve our full potential. It may take time and effort to establish these habits, but the benefits they bring are well worth the investment. So let us continue to cultivate these habits and reap the rewards of a more fulfilling and successful life.

- Final thoughts on the journey to success

Success is a journey that looks different for everyone, but one thing is certain - it is not a destination but rather a continuous process of growth and improvement. As we reflect on our own personal journeys to success, it is important to acknowledge the challenges and setbacks we faced along the way. These obstacles are not failures but rather opportunities for learning and development. By overcoming these challenges, we gain valuable experience and insight that ultimately propel us forward on our path to success.

It is important to remember that success is not defined by external factors such as wealth, status, or accolades. True success is about achieving personal fulfillment and satisfaction in our endeavors. This may look different for everyone - for some, success may mean landing their dream job, while for others it may mean starting their own business or making a positive impact on their community. Whatever success looks like for you, it is essential to stay true to your values and beliefs throughout the journey.

One of the key aspects of achieving success is setting clear goals and creating a plan to reach them. Goals provide a sense of direction and purpose, motivating us to take action and move closer towards our desired outcome. It is important to set both short-term and long-term goals to keep us on track and ensure that we are making progress towards our vision of success. However, it is also important to remain flexible and adapt our goals as needed to reflect changes in our circumstances or priorities.

Another crucial component of success is cultivating a growth mindset. A growth mindset is the belief that our abilities and intelligence are not fixed traits but can be developed through effort, perseverance, and learning. By embracing a growth mindset, we are more likely to see setbacks and challenges as opportunities for growth rather than insurmountable obstacles. This mindset allows us to approach new challenges with courage and resilience, knowing that we have the capacity to overcome them through dedication and hard work.

Building a strong support network is also essential on the journey to success. Surrounding ourselves with positive and supportive individuals who believe in our potential can provide us with the encouragement and motivation we need to keep pushing forward. Whether it is friends, family, mentors, or colleagues, having a strong support system can help us navigate the ups and downs of our journey and provide valuable insight and advice when needed. It is important to set clear goals, cultivate a growth mindset, and build a strong support network to help us overcome challenges and achieve our desired outcomes. Success is not a destination but rather a continuous journey of self-improvement and personal growth. By staying true to our values and beliefs, and remaining committed to our goals, we can navigate the ups and downs of our journey with resilience and determination. Ultimately, success is not about reaching a specific destination but rather about the personal fulfillment and satisfaction we gain along the way.

9 798224 764471